The Modern Short Story

Frank Myszor

Series Editor: Adrian Barlow

CAMBRIDGE
UNIVERSITY PRESS

PUBLISHED BY THE PRESS SYNDICATE OF THE UNIVERSITY OF CAMBRIDGE
The Pitt Building, Trumpington Street, Cambridge, United Kingdom

CAMBRIDGE UNIVERSITY PRESS
The Edinburgh Building, Cambridge CB2 2RU, UK
40 West 20th Street, New York, NY 10011–4211, USA
10 Stamford Road, Oakleigh, VIC 3166, Australia
Ruiz de Alarcón 13, 28014 Madrid, Spain
Dock House, The Waterfront, Cape Town 8001, South Africa

http://www.cambridge.org

First published 2001

Printed in the United Kingdom at the University Press, Cambridge

Typefaces: Clearface and Mixage   *System:* QuarkXPress® 4.1

A catalogue record for this book is available from the British Library

ISBN 0 521 77473 X paperback

Prepared for publication by Gill Stacey
Designed by Tattersall Hammarling & Silk
Cover: *Merry-Go-Round 1916* by Mark Gertler.
Oil on canvas 189.3 x 142.2 © Tate, London 2000

Contents

Introduction

The modern short story has suffered critical neglect in Britain. In countless histories of English literature it is not mentioned at all, squeezed out somewhere in between the novel and poetry. In educational books, short stories tend to be swallowed up by the novel, as if all prose works are to be studied in the same way. That neglect denies the important role played by short stories in the history of literature written in English. This book is something of an attempt to redress the situation by examining short stories in the following contexts:

- historical, cultural and social
- writing by the same author
- writing by other authors of the same period
- literary movements
- developments in other artistic forms

In America and other English-speaking countries short stories are treated quite differently from Britain. America has championed short stories since they were defined by Edgar Allan Poe in the 1840s. They have since become something of an institution, supported at various times by America's need to define its own society, by a thriving magazine culture, by writing manuals and workshops. This book focuses for the most part on these two extremes: short stories written in English mainly in Britain and America. Other English-speaking countries such as Canada and the Caribbean are also taken into consideration. In Part 1, where historical roots are explored, there is a brief excursion into short stories not originally written in English, namely into the work of Anton Chekhov, a Russian, and Guy de Maupassant, a Frenchman. These are the only exceptions to the rule, deemed necessary because of the importance of these two writers to a history of the genre.

America has become somewhat obsessed by the search for a definition of the modern short story. Everyone knows what a story is. So it should be startlingly obvious what a short story is, give or take some argument about how short it has to be. But in this book the term 'modern short story' has a precise meaning: it refers to fictional stories written primarily as art and usually published in journals, newspapers, magazines and anthologies over the last 200 years. Here are some non-qualifiers, even though they are clearly stories and are usually short:

- traditional fairy tales (although modern rewritings of these do count)
- newspaper reports
- stories told by friends in pubs

- jokes that tell stories

- television news items

- diary entries

- the parables of the Bible

Most of these story forms have had some influence on the modern short story at some point in its history. Several of them are derived from oral stories – the earliest form of story – and continue to find their way into the modern written form. Stories with a moral such as parables and some fairy tales featured strongly in early tales of the 18th and early 19th century. Anecdotes and jokes are, like many short stories, dependent on the ending for their impact. But such end-loaded stories peaked in terms of artistic credibility in the late 19th century and have since largely come to be seen as popular entertainment. In recent years the modern short story has borrowed from these forms as it has become more diverse in its methods. Indeed, an interesting question to have arisen in recent years is whether the modern short story is still a single genre or lots of different ones.

Perhaps surprisingly, the 'modern' of the modern short story is easier to define than the 'short'. The phrase 'the modern short story' generally refers to works written after about 1840 up to the present time, although there is some argument for choosing the later date of 1880. The earliest good examples of the form were written by Russians such as Nikolai Gogol (1809–1852) and Americans such as Nathaniel Hawthorne (1804–1864) and Edgar Allan Poe (1809–1849). The latter played an important part in recognising that a new literary form was appearing and set out to define it in his critical writing. English writers of the time such as Jane Austen and Charles Dickens also wrote short stories but were, of course, better known for their novels and played little part in the development of the modern short story.

Discussions about the length of short stories are fraught with confusion. Some novels (Steinbeck's *Of Mice and Men*) are unusually short whereas some short stories, particularly those by Henry James (*The Turn of the Screw*) or Alice Munro are almost novels. Whatever defines it, the modern short story is more than just a story that is short. Usually, short stories can be digested in a single sitting and this may have to do as a working definition. Inevitably, the short story is compared, favourably or otherwise, with the novel, as in these two opinions:

> ... whether it sprawls or neatly bites its own tail, a short story is a concept that the writer can 'hold', fully realised, in his imagination, at one time. A novel is, by comparison, staked out, and must be taken possession of stage by stage; it is impossible to contain, all at once ...
> (Nadine Gordimer Introduction to *Selected Stories*, 1975)

I am inclined to think that the short story is usually a waste of a good novel: by the time the setting and the characters have been set up, it is almost time to leave them.

(Anthony Burgess *Flame into Being*, 1985)

How the book is organised

Part 1: Putting short stories in their place

Part 1 is a survey of approximately two centuries of the modern short story. It divides into three sections: 19th-century short stories; modernist stories, covering the first few decades of the 20th century; contemporary and post-modern stories, dealing with developments since the Second World War.

Part 2: Approaching the texts

This part looks at the range of techniques used by short story writers.

Part 3: Stories and extracts

Part 3 contains stories and extracts discussed in the rest of the book and used as the focus of many of the assignments. The selection contains important and well-known stories, as well as the less widely known.

Part 4: Critical approaches

This part looks at theoretical approaches to the short story as a distinct genre.

Part 5: How to write about short stories

This part offers practical assistance for writing about short stories in context.

Part 6: Resources

This part provides further reading lists, a glossary, a chronology of short stories in their historical context, and an index.

Terms that appear in the glossary are highlighted in bold when they first appear in the main text.

Throughout this book and at the ends of Parts 1, 2, 4 and 5, there are tasks and assignments designed to address the issues raised in the text.

1 | Putting short stories in their place

Part 1 describes the development of modern short stories during three main periods: the 19th century; the modernist era (1900–1930); the contemporary and post-modern era (1960 to the present). The following questions will be addressed:

- Why did modern short stories emerge in the 19th century?

- What are the important features of short stories?

- How have short stories changed?

- How have literary movements influenced short stories?

- How have significant writers developed the form?

Short stories in the 19th century

The roots of modern short stories

It has been argued that modern short stories came into existence between 1830 and 1850, but influences can be traced back several decades before that. Gothic writing began with the novel *The Castle of Otranto* (1764) by Horace Walpole and reached its peak at the beginning of the 19th century. Today this writing would be called 'horror' but it also became a way of exploring scientific developments, for example in the understanding of electricity – which some people thought was the key to the creation of life. Gothic was important in the development of the short story because it was the genre practised by two early short story writers, both American: Nathaniel Hawthorne (1804–1864) and Edgar Allan Poe (1809–1849). Gothic style has continued to influence short stories to the present day (for example, in the work of Joyce Carol Oates), but some critics argue that the short story as we know it today did not emerge until **realism** (see page 23) took over from gothic as a dominant influence.

Like gothic writing, Romanticism was a reaction against the thinking of the 18th century, which had been known as the age of reason. In the first half of the 19th century Romanticism dominated poetry, with its emphasis on imagination. Romantic poetry often recounted moments of insight or revelation, particularly in the poetry of William Wordsworth, but it was several decades before this feature became apparent in short stories. Romanticism's favourite themes included childhood and the exiled hero, with all forms of authoritarian government being rejected. Some critics therefore claim that short stories echo the spirit of Romanticism because they speak for the isolated individual, the outcast, the little man cast against the wildness and lawlessness of society or against the vast power of the state machine – these last two points applying to 19th-century America and Russia respectively. This claim is supported by publishing history, at least in America, where the short story has often been a mouthpiece for previously unrecognised writers who represent a local region or a local dialect.

If modern short stories came into existence between 1830 and 1850, what came before and how was this different from what came after? According to some critics the short story originates from **tales** and **sketches**, although it would be wrong to expect a clear cut-off point after which only short stories were written. Poetry and novels were, of course, well-established literary forms by this time, novels more so in Britain than America, and although they can be treated separately in historical terms, both of them exerted some influence over the development of short stories.

Tales are distinguished by the dominance of the following features:

- **plot** – in the sense of a series of actions leading to a conclusion
- a moral – which was often 'tagged' onto the end
- caricatures – rather than fully formed characters, these were types
- sentimentalism – tales were often designed to arouse feelings in the reader in an obvious and unsubtle way.

Two important collections of tales were Washington Irving's confusingly titled *Sketch Book* (1820) and Hawthorne's *Twice Told Tales* (1842). Irving's work actually contains both tales and sketches, but the most memorable are the tales. 'The Legend of Sleepy Hollow', effectively a ghost story, and 'Rip Van Winkle', about a man who falls asleep for 20 years, have entered American folklore because they vividly create a sense of place and because, with the plot dominating, they read rather like folk tales.

A second kind of earlier short form was the sketch. Here a writer would write about an experience, fictional or semi-fictional, in order to make a point, just as an essay might use narrative to illustrate a point. Sketches in the form of essays were associated with writers such as Joseph Addison (1672–1719) and Richard Steele (1672–1729) who wrote in the journal, *The Spectator*. Later, in the 19th century, sketches became descriptive fragments which, linked together, often created a vivid picture of a time and place. The best-known were Dickens' *Sketches by Boz* (1835–1836) and Thackeray's *The Book of Snobs* (1846).

Under the influence of the ideas of Edgar Allan Poe, critics in the mid-19th century began to reject stories that were just stories – plot and little else. The idea that short stories should concentrate on creating a single impression in the reader had also begun to take hold, and so embellishments were rejected as unnecessary. Critics began to favour a more economic style of writing. However, this change of taste did not mean that plots suddenly disappeared overnight. In fact, stories that led to a twist in the tale were seen as creating a single impression because everything in the story led up to that crucial moment. Another significant development was that short stories began to work by means of suggestion rather than explicit statement of a point, although it was to be many years before this feature was consistently adopted. This happened at different rates in different countries, Russia being one of the first, in the stories of Nikolai Gogol (1809–1852) and Ivan Turgenev (1818–1883), especially in Turgenev's *The Sportsman's Sketches* (1846).

▶ Identify the features of tales in the story 'Crazy Robin' (Part 3, pages 73–76). How explicit is the moral of this story?

Short stories and novels in Britain and America

It would be difficult for two countries to differ as radically as Britain and America with respect to short stories. In 19th-century America short stories flourished; in Britain they played a secondary role to the dominant form, the novel. Many critics claimed that the short story was America's national literary form. ('As opera was to Italy, the short story was to America', Shapard and Thomas *Sudden Fiction*, 1986.) This rather exaggerated claim was possibly an attempt at literary independence, given that America could not compete with England where the novel was concerned. It is true that the early great writers of the short story in English were American: Hawthorne, Irving (1783–1859) and Poe for example. But why should this be so?

America in the 19th century

America in the 19th century has been described as a 'melting pot' – in the sense that it was a society emerging from the many nations that had settled there. Throughout most of the century America had effectively been at war with its Native American population and most of the continent was still unexplored wilderness. The War of Independence (1775–1783) had laid down the principles for this new society but most of the 19th century was spent trying to put them into practice and the Civil War in the 1860s was a further destabilisation. America's traditions were less well established than Britain's, so it was much more likely to support a literature that was immediate, accessible and egalitarian. Perhaps the short story was the form best suited to a society that was still fragmented and striving for equality. After all, short stories were easier to publish and could represent lots of small, individual voices striving to be heard.

But why should America have been so rich in short stories? The answer lies in the explosion in magazine culture, especially in the second half of the 19th century. The situation was later aided by changes in the copyright laws which made it difficult for magazine publishers to import material from Britain. Tom Verde writes:

> During the mid to late 19th century, literature in America was largely a preoccupation of the privileged East coast society. It explored upper class values, was often sentimental and overloaded with conventional morality. Stylistically, it was as stuffy and ornate as the Victorian drawing rooms where it was meant to be read aloud. For the most part it was unrealistic and out of touch with the sweeping changes that were occurring in the American landscape, such as the rapid growth of cities and industry, and the bold, sweeping settlement of the western half of the country.
>
> A few publishers, however, began to recognise that there was a huge, untapped reading market in the working class, and so a new breed of popular magazine was born. Inexpensive, packed with short stories, serialisations and features, these magazines catered to the tastes of the man on the street.
>
> (Tom Verde *Twentieth Century Writers 1900–1950*, 1998)

Britain in the 19th century

In many ways 19th-century Britain was ideal for the novel. The basis for modern industrial society was established in England during the Victorian Age (1837–1901). Railways, for example, were built and there was an enormous rise in the population of the cities. The empire was huge and powerful, industry was rapidly expanding and there was an air of confidence. This was perfectly suited to a literature that was large in scope, both in terms of the times and places portrayed and the sheer length of the novels. Even the poets of the age, such as Tennyson and Browning, produced works of epic proportions. The success of the English novel in the 19th century arose from a society ideally suited to support it.

These then were the key reasons why, compared with other countries, Britain was a 'late starter' in short story writing and publishing. But this obviously does not mean that no short stories were written. The great English novelists – Charles Dickens, Thomas Hardy, Elizabeth Gaskell – also wrote short stories, but their work was neither substantial nor ground-breaking.

1842

1842 was arguably a seminal year in the history of modern short stories. First, in that year the American writer Edgar Allan Poe made definitive statements about the nature of short stories in his review of Nathaniel Hawthorne's *Twice Told Tales*. Poe was a theorist of the short story whose statements about the nature of the form have become an important defining moment. But he was also a practitioner whose gothic stories of the macabre enjoyed considerable popularity whilst exemplifying his own theories. Second, the Russian writer Nikolai Gogol wrote his celebrated story 'The Overcoat' which set the pattern for the form to follow. 'The Overcoat' tells the story of an ordinary man who wants to get his overcoat repaired. The story is important because it anticipated much of what was to come: it is about an apparently ordinary event in the life of an insignificant person; it is written without commentary from the narrator and it is an early example of realism (see page 23).

Edgar Allan Poe

Edgar Allan Poe (1809–1849) is best known in the popular imagination for his much filmed stories of the macabre. In literary circles, he is better known for having defined the modern short story. However, the two facts should not be seen in isolation from each other: both resulted from a passion for the promotion of a magazine culture devoted to short stories. In 1837, Poe began to see 'the magazine, rather than the book, as the appropriate expression of American culture'. For Poe the short story was closely tied to commercial interests, sharing several of the properties of the medium in which it should appear: magazines were, after all, quickly produced, easily digestible and disposable. With commercial enterprise becoming the driving force behind American culture, the short story seemed the ideal way of packaging literature. In this respect Poe was perhaps ahead of his time. To some extent there was also a political side to his dream of a magazine devoted to short stories. Such a magazine would offer more independence for American writers who were competing with serialised novels imported from Britain. This new form would then be associated with the New World, shaking off the outmoded forms of writing associated with the Old World.

Poe worked within the gothic tradition which he successfully transferred from novel to short story form. Gothic writing employed settings and symbols such as medieval castles, graveyards, instruments of torture and bizarre scientific experiments. Gothic novels had reached the height of their success in the late 18th century into the early 19th century in works such as Mary Shelley's *Frankenstein* (1818), and influenced later 19th-century novels such as those by Emily Brontë and Charles Dickens. During the first half of the 19th century, the time was ripe for such morbid and pseudo-scientific imaginings: scientific and other kinds of discoveries began to open up vast possibilities for the unknown – a trend that continued throughout the century and thus ensured Poe's lasting popularity. In this respect the subjects of Poe's stories differed from those of 20th century short story writers, who tended towards the mundane rather than the extraordinary.

Typically, Poe wrote about individuals isolated in time and space from the rest of the world, usually by some monstrous predicament. For example, for most of 'The Pit and the Pendulum' (1843) a man is trapped in a dungeon in which a massive razor-sharp pendulum is slowly descending to slice him in two; in 'The Cask of Amontillado' (1846) a man is set on killing a rival by incarcerating him in his sherry vaults; 'The Tell-Tale Heart' (1845) is set almost entirely in one room as a man sets about killing another and is eventually questioned by the police on the very same spot. These situations, physically enclosed and intensely focused on one man's crisis, made it easy for Poe to create what he called '**unity of impression**' – stories in which every element contributes to some overall atmosphere or idea.

The psychological side of this isolation was clearly paramount to Poe's stories and it is perhaps this feature which influenced subsequent writers the most. What has changed, especially in 20th-century writing, is the way in which that isolation is created. Poe's stories were precise, almost mathematical in their description of physical surroundings, and intense in their evocation of terror. Later writers came to put more emphasis on the effect of mundane or symbolic moments on people's lives. But Poe's influence as a practitioner and a theorist of short stories is probably more significant than that of any other writer in English. For some critics, Poe's short stories are also the basis for the claim that Poe is the father of the science fiction genre.

▶ Using any two stories by Poe, examine the ways in which Poe creates 'unity of impression'. You may wish to consider the physical setting and point of view. To what extent to you feel that Poe succeeds in achieving this unity?

Guy de Maupassant

Guy de Maupassant (1850–1893) wrote six novels, but his short stories are regarded as his greatest achievements and it is for these that he is best known. His stories were often set in rural Normandy in northern France, and dealt with themes such as adultery, humiliated women and jilted men, prostitution, the Franco-Prussian War and the cunning of the peasants. His most famous stories are 'Boule de Suif' (1880) and 'The Necklace' (1885). His short stories are characterised by strong plots, and the classic twist in the tale. 'The Necklace', for example, is the story of a poor woman who borrows a necklace from a rich friend in order to attend a society function. The necklace is lost, the woman spends years of hardship saving for a replacement, only to discover, finally, that the original was an imitation and worth nothing at all. Those who dislike his stories have called them nationalistic and chauvinistic – indeed the latter accords with Maupassant's reputation as a sexual athlete.

Maupassant prompted much debate about the idea of the 'twist in the tale' – a notion that remains important in the interpretation of modern short stories. For many readers Maupassant's technique was so skilful that it masked a lack of substance in his stories – stories that merely trick the reader rather than develop any substantial theme. A similar argument follows from Maupassant's skill as an observer; this ability translates itself so seamlessly into objective writing (in which only outwardly observable things are described) that it is easy to doubt Maupassant's authenticity – to suggest that he is unable to reflect on his characters' inner lives and is therefore something of a sham.

The first of these criticisms can be answered by asking if his stories can stand a second reading. If they cannot, then it is because the secret revealed at the end is the only thing that makes the story worth telling: once this is known the whole power of the story is lost. In the case of 'The Necklace' and many others, the final twist does in fact serve a thematic purpose as well as a narrative one. The revelation that the necklace is a fake and therefore not worth striving to replace serves to reinforce Maupassant's pessimistic philosophy – that human striving can be defeated by merely random events. The second criticism – the suspicion aroused by his objective writing – perhaps requires less of an answer today than when Maupassant was alive. Objective writing has since become the norm rather than the exception, especially with regard to the short story. This is typified (and taken to new extremes) by the work of Ernest Hemingway in the early years of the 20th century. A lack of reflection or extensive comment was one of the significant features that began to distinguish the short story from the full length novel.

Anton Chekhov

If Poe was the godfather of the modern short story, then Anton Chekhov (1860–1904) was the father. Chekhov was a Russian writer better known for his plays, above all *Uncle Vanya* (1897), *The Three Sisters* (1901) and *The Cherry Orchard* (1904). His best short stories were the 60 he published between 1888 and 1904, including 'Ward Number Six' (1893) 'A Dreary Story' (1890), 'Ariadne' (1895) and 'The Butterfly' (1894).

It would scarcely be possible to find a writer whose subject matter and style differed so much from that of Poe. It should come as no surprise that at the beginning of the 19th century, the American continent, still to a large extent unexplored, should produce a very different kind of writing from that produced by the European continent, the seat of civilisation for centuries. Thus, H.E. Bates, the English short story writer, called American 19th-century short story writing 'raw, facile, journalistic, prosy, cheap'. European writing (which includes Russian) had, by contrast, all of the trappings and sophistication of civilisation. Neither did Russian stories conform to the features of short stories described by Poe, having evolved from a tradition begun by other Russian writers such as Gogol and Turgenev.

Chekhov frequently dwelt on the ordinary, and was the first real exponent of what has become known as the '**slice of life**' story – almost plotless and focusing on the psychological reality of one or two ordinary characters. His most frequent theme was the relationship between men and women. 'Lady with Lapdog' (1899) deals with an affair between a middle-aged gigolo and a young married woman. It is a highly sensitive account of the intense emotions associated with the affair, focusing in particular on the man's change from casual to committed lover. 'Grief' (1885) mixes comedy and tragedy in its description of an old man's attempts to take his dying wife to the doctor. During the journey the reader is given a profile of a failed relationship and its tragic effect on both partners. Typically, these stories create mood and atmosphere rather than plot, so that a superficial reading of Chekhov's work can give the impression that 'nothing ever happens'.

Chekhov was able to deal with a range of characters, reflecting perhaps his own beginnings as the son of a grocer and his rise to the middle classes as a doctor of medicine. But like many 19th-century short story writers he paid a great deal of attention to the lower classes – something which short stories were more likely to do than the novel, especially in the Russian tradition following Gogol. Chekhov's work sometimes dealt in a general sense with the decline of Russian society in the decades before the Communist Revolution in 1917, but he showed no obvious commitment to any particular political or philosophical point of view. It was as a stylist that he most influenced 20th-century short story writers.

Charles Dickens

Charles Dickens' (1812–1870) first contribution to English literature is, of course, his novels. As a writer of short stories his merit is debatable. His first novel was *The Pickwick Papers* (1836–1837), but before that he wrote sketches – short portraits of London life and characters – published under the title *Sketches by Boz* (1836). This collection included his first proper short story, 'The Black Veil', inspired by a visit to a prison and with a 'twist in the tale' ending. Thereafter his short stories were closely connected with his journalistic work as the editor of the magazines *Household Words* and *All the Year Round*. Dickens wrote five Christmas books (of which *A Christmas Carol* is the most enduring) taken from special Christmas editions of his magazine. 'The Signalman', his best-known and most highly praised story, appeared in the 1866 edition, but it is rarely read in its original context of the story sequence 'Mugby Junction'.

For its modern readers 'The Signalman' has no associations with Christmas, although it was written in the tradition of fireside ghost story telling that was so important to Victorian families. This points to one of the ways in which critics have judged Dickens' short stories. Many have dismissed his contribution because his relaxed style is so much at odds with the **compression** and omission of the style that came to prevail in the 20th century. It is also worth remembering that Dickens wrote at a time when the division between the literary short story and the popular story was blurred, so it is easy to see his stories as journalism rather than serious writing. Another reason for this neglect is that ghost stories rarely feature as serious writing today. A.S. Byatt's 'The July Ghost' (in *Sugar and Other Stories*, 1987) is a worthy exception.

The critic Alastair Fowler assesses Dickens in another way. He sees Dickens in terms of **short story cycles** – collections of interconnected short stories that create an impression of a place. So, for example, the fragments in *Sketches by Boz* created a popular image of London. Later Christmas editions experimented with ways of linking stories, such as in 'Mugby Junction' (1886). Sometimes, for example, the connection between stories was an object that had appeared in one of the stories, and then reappeared in others.

Thomas Hardy

Like Dickens, Thomas Hardy (1840–1928) is one of the best-known English novelists, but he also published several volumes of short stories. He did not develop the form in any significant way, although his stories may be regarded as a landmark for a particular kind of story. His most famous stories include 'The Distracted Preacher' (1879), 'The Withered Arm' (1888) and 'The Melancholy Hussar of the German Legion' (1894). His best-known collections are *Wessex Tales: Strange, Lively and Commonplace* (1888) and *Life's Little Ironies* (1894).

Although they were first published in magazines, many of Hardy's stories imitate an oral form, in which a narrator tells a story in front of a gathered audience. Hardy's attitude to his subject matter contrasts significantly with the attitude of the later modernists (see page 30). Hardy felt that 'A story must be exceptional enough to justify its telling.' Consequently his stories were often tragic love triangles or ghost stories, some of which he took from local folklore. Hardy frequently gave the impression that his stories were genuine folklore by ending with statements such as 'But the arrival of the three strangers at the shepherd's that night … is a story as well known as ever in the country about Higher Crowstairs.' For these reasons many critics regard his stories as little more than anecdotes, which typically end with a twist or a revelation of circumstances explaining the events of the story (as in 'The Three Strangers', 1883). In most respects Hardy's short stories represent a conservative form associated with the label 'tales'.

H.E. Bates felt that Hardy's style was too expansive (his novels are usually very long) to suit the short story form and that he did not change his style to suit the requirements of short story writing. However, it is worth remembering that the 19th-century practice of serialising both short stories and novels did not help to develop the compression of style that came to mark later stories. In spite of all this, there are features of Hardy's short stories that look to the future. First, Hardy used places and objects as symbols, a feature that would increase in popularity as compression became more and more the accepted style. Secondly, Hardy used his stories to question social institutions such as marriage. Many 19th-century novels had ended with marriage, suggesting that this was morally the 'right' outcome, but Hardy reversed this 'right' ending in stories such as 'The Melancholy Hussar of the German Legion'.

▶ To what extent do you agree with the views of H.E. Bates and the others given above? Test out these ideas by comparing the openings of short stories and novels by Hardy. An example of each can be found in Part 3, page 71 (Extract 2) and page 73 (Extract 7).

Robert Louis Stevenson

Robert Louis Stevenson (1850–1894) is regarded as one of the few writers in Britain to make an impact on the short story form before Rudyard Kipling. Stevenson wrote horror stories similar to Poe's in that they concentrate on a solitary character in a predicament, often in some kind of moral dilemma. In 'Markheim' (1887), for example, a man who has just killed an antique dealer encounters the devil while still in the house of his victim. Some of Stevenson's stories are set in the South Pacific, where he lived for some years.

Rather like Kipling, Stevenson's contribution to the short story is often overlooked, even though he wrote several volumes. This is largely because much of his more famous work cannot easily be categorised, but also because as a writer he was very uneven. Although he wrote novels – *Kidnapped* (1886) and *Treasure Island* (1883) – these works are seen as belonging to the popular adventure genre and are seldom taken as seriously as the realism that was produced in such vast quantities during the 19th century. His other successful works, *The Strange Case of Dr Jekyll and Mr Hyde* (1886) and 'The Beach of Falesa' (1893), were novellas. The former became a popular story immortalised by Hollywood, an established part of popular psychology and a classic of the gothic genre. An additional problem for most 20th-century readers is that some of Stevenson's best stories (such as 'Thrawn Janet', 1887) were written in Scots dialect.

In spite of appearances Stevenson took his art very seriously. He seemed to understand the short story in a way that almost made him 20th-century. He saw, for example, the importance of endings and their connection with beginnings. Like Poe, unity was all important: for Stevenson, not one word should be wasted in contributing to the overall design of the story. He saw that the essence of story should be in action rather than description, anticipating the modern distinction between showing and telling (see page 57) and the later pre-eminence of the former. Stylish writing that was elaborate or 'showy' was not what the short story needed – it just needed to be clear. Again this sounds like the 20th-century idea of suggestion through the use of significant and vivid images. He also believed that the moral should not be tagged on at the end, but should be present throughout the whole story. In spite of these advanced views, his stories did not always match up to his theory. Some critics think that the style of his stories looked backwards more than forwards and that ultimately, as is revealed in his longer and popular works, his faith in the power of story telling separates him from the modernism that was to emerge shortly after his death.

Rudyard Kipling

Rudyard Kipling (1865–1936) was an Englishman who spent much of his life abroad, especially in India, and it is the experiences of those places that coloured his stories. He has been immortalised by his children's stories, *The Jungle Books* (1894–1895) and *Just So Stories* (1902), and to a lesser extent by his one successful novel, *Kim* (1901). All are characterised by their exotic location. But it is as a short story writer that Kipling receives most praise in literary circles, and it is usually in the following context. Critics point out that England was without a great short story writer for most of the 19th century until Kipling wrote *Plain Tales from the Hills* in 1888. A possible explanation for this is that, in England, fiction was dominated by the full-length novel, a form that had been developed to world-wide success by authors such as Charles Dickens and Thomas Hardy. This explanation is made more likely by the fact that throughout the 19th century most novels were published serially in periodicals, thus increasing the level of direct competition between novel and short story, which was also published in serial form.

Although there is no doubting the quality and range of Kipling's short stories (and he continued to develop his art for several decades), their impact is often obscured by the popularity of his children's books and by the often controversial nature of his writing about India and South Africa. In short, Kipling's right wing views, expressed in military settings that caricatured the working class, and which were unsympathetic to women, have for some time made him an unfashionable writer. He began writing at a time when such views did not prevent his work from being a popular success in both India and England. But when attitudes changed after the First World War, his readership declined rapidly.

In contrast to this over-patriotic content, Kipling's contribution to the stylistic development of the short story was rather un-English. For much of the 19th century the short story stood in contrast to the verbosity and moral weightiness of the novel. That is, where novels could expand, short stories compressed, so that the novelist's tendency to interrupt the story to comment on a philosophical issue or to give an opinion of a character was a feature absent, by and large, from short stories. Another feature of novels' expansiveness was in the use of vocabulary derived from Latin or extravagantly poetic imagery. For example, Hardy writes 'As the sun passed the meridian and declined westward' when he could have said 'the sun began to set'. Short stories of this time, particularly in America, were far more likely than novels to use plain English, or rather to use language that was closer to spoken English. Kipling, however, was an exception in Britain, his narrators often appearing to be anti-literary in style and sometimes representing the voice of the common soldier. In this respect, he echoed American short story writers such as Bret Harte (1836–1902) and Stephen Crane (1871–1900), using a style he had developed as a journalist in daily contact with ordinary soldiers in India.

'Mrs Bathurst' (1904) is one of Kipling's most acclaimed short stories. It tells the story of a sailor's obsessive love for Mrs Bathurst through the eyes of two other men. But the story's importance lies not so much in its subject matter as in the style of its telling. It consists of a series of narrative fragments that the reader reconstructs into a coherent story. In this respect it seemed to be ahead of its time, anticipating the fragmented style of writing that would typify experimental work much later in the 20th century (for example, by Jorge Luis Borges). The story also seemed to be influenced by techniques used in film – one of the basic principles of editing is the combination of apparently disconnected 'shots' to form a coherent whole. This technique was probably used consciously by Kipling – the story itself contains one of the earliest ever references to film as a central image. Many writers have claimed that it is no coincidence that the beginnings of the modern short story and the beginnings of film occur at around the same time in history.

▶ 'Crazy Robin' and the extract from 'Lispeth' (Part 3, pages 73–76 and 80–81) were written about 100 years apart. Explore the differences in style, particularly in the way that the two authors evoke emotion towards the end. To what extent do you agree that Kipling uses a style that is simpler and more direct?

The legacy of the 19th century

The work of Poe, Chekhov, Maupassant and Kipling shows the main features that were to determine the progress of the short story in the 20th century. These features can be summarised as follows, though it should be emphasised that this is a highly schematic account of these writers' contributions:

• Poe – unity of effect, the bizarre

- Chekhov – plotlessness, character and situation
- Maupassant – objective narration and end-loaded plots
- Kipling – fragmentation of narrative, the influence of journalism

A further arrangement of these names is possible. Poe represents the formal beginning of the genre of the short story. Kipling provides a bridge between the 19th and 20th centuries, not just because his lifetime spanned the two, but because his style developed to encompass new ways of thinking about presenting stories. Chekhov and Maupassant were almost exact contemporaries, born within ten years of each other, but representing the two poles of short story writing that were to develop extensively in the next century. Maupassant represents the end-loaded, plot-centred story with the twist in the tale, popularised at almost the same time in America by O. Henry and reaching a mass audience in, for example, the tales of Roald Dahl in the 1970s and 1980s.

At least two of these writers illustrate a common circumstance for writers of short stories. Both Chekhov and Kipling were overshadowed by their other literary achievements; for Chekhov it was plays, for Kipling his children's stories, and arguably Poe's fame as a short story writer rests on the American film industry as much as on the power of his writing. Only Maupassant's short stories outshone his novels. This situation arises from the short story's status as a literary form. It is often seen as the form of apprenticeship, associated with artists' formative years in which they cut their literary teeth before moving on to greater achievements. A similar status is bestowed by the resulting economic associations: short stories are seen as the means by which budding, struggling or hack writers make their money.

Short stories and the commercial world

It is often claimed that short stories are more strongly connected with the commercial world than other literary genres. This claim derives from the short story's association with struggling writers, or, as in William Faulkner's case, with the need to quickly make enough money to attempt a major work such as a novel. Short stories have always been published primarily in magazines and newspapers, with anthologies a secondary consideration, often with the publisher's profits rather than the writer's in mind.

Serialisation also played an interesting part in the development of novels and short stories during the 19th century. The century's prominent writers often serialised their novels in magazines and this had a considerable effect on the way that they were written. It meant that writers could be in touch with their readers as they were writing, by means of the many letters that authors such as Dickens received. This in turn meant that they were able to respond to their readers' tastes, the famous example of this being that Dickens changed the ending of *Great Expectations* in response to the opinions of a friend. It is less well-known that 19th-century short stories were also serialised, particularly longer works like those by Hardy and Henry James. To some extent, this worked against Poe's idea that the short story should convey a single idea, and that everything should aim at promoting that single idea. If a short story was divided into two or three parts, as was often the case, then the intensity of the story was likely to be severely reduced.

▶ Investigate the effects of serialisation on the stories of Hardy and James. Two good starting points are the books by Levi and Shaw (see Further reading, page 119).

There are other important commercial influences on the development of the genre. When Poe first defined the modern short story, he attempted to promote and establish it through his own magazine. Magazines, in contrast to books, appealed to Americans because they provided more opportunities for publication, especially for previously unpublished writers. Magazines, and by association short stories, were therefore seen as egalitarian – as speaking for the ordinary person. These were ideas associated with the kind of society that Americans were attempting to create; that is, one with opportunities for all. Commercial factors combined to make the short story particularly strong in America when copyright laws were changed in the 1890s. These changes prevented American magazines from publishing British novels and so they were obliged to publish more work by American writers. A few decades later, the proliferation of short story manuals, explaining how to write stories, played a similar part in promoting the form. In view of this, it is not surprising that many Americans regard the short story as their national art form. Thus, commercial considerations played an important part in making short stories what they are.

Realism and short stories

Some theorists see the short story as intimately linked with the rise of realism in the 19th century. Realism is notoriously difficult to define, but, beyond the obvious implications of the word, it is useful to consider what realism is not:

- Realism is not romance, in which there may be an exaggerated quest for some ideal.

- Realism is not gothic in which the darker reaches of our psyches are explored by means of now familiar images such as haunted houses, ravens and thunderstorms.

- Realism is not fantasy, in which a man may fall asleep for 20 years.

In short, realism deals with moments from everyday life and was defined as 'truth to the observed facts (especially when they are gloomy)' (Paul Harvey *The Oxford Companion to English Literature,* 1932). In some artistic forms this was not seen as appropriate subject matter, as, for example, when mid-19th-century French artists shocked the public by portraying ordinary people in their paintings.

This shift towards realism in 19th-century writing may have been influenced by the development of still photography which was invented in 1826 and made public as a process in 1839. The ability to represent reality with apparent precision may have influenced the verbal arts. In America, the Civil War (1861–1865) also contributed to the development of realism when writers such as Stephen Crane and Ambrose Bierce (1842–1914) sought to capture psychological truth in their short stories.

In the 1860s another movement in fine art may have influenced short stories. Painters such as Monet began to use brush strokes to emphasise the impression created in the eye of the observer. A collection of crude brush marks might, for example, combine to create the impression of a complete object. In the same way, writers of short stories began to create an impression of reality not by describing scenes in minute detail (as was typical of the novel), but by revealing fragments from which the full story could be built up by the reader. This applies particularly well to Kipling's 'Mrs Bathurst', which comprises a series of fragments provided by the narrator (see page 21).

Another factor that aided the move towards realism was that, in the second half of the 19th century, America was still a fragmented country with many authors writing in magazines about the place in which they lived. Thus, many writers at this time were **local colourists** – meaning that they created an image and identity for the place in which they lived by setting many of their stories in that place. Examples of this kind of writing were Kate Chopin, who wrote about French communities living in the far South, and, in the 20th century, Sherwood Anderson, whose connected stories, *Winesburg, Ohio* (1919), were highly influential over a generation of writers.

This association with realism allowed the short story to break more decisively with influences such as the gothic, the ghost story and the folk tale. Poe's gothic was sensational, Hawthorne's tended to be moralistic; and ghost stories and folk tales promoted plot-centred stories with neat endings. Once these elements disappeared, the short story could concentrate on the more mundane but authentic aspects of everyday life.

Women's voices: Gilman, Wharton and Chopin

Towards the end of the 19th century the traditional position of women in western society became more and more difficult to sustain; for example, until 1882 women in Britain had no legal control over their own earned income. Inevitably, these feelings were expressed in the literature of the time. In the years leading to the end of the century, three writers, all American, wrote short stories that expressed these inequalities: Charlotte Perkins Gilman (1860–1935), Edith Wharton (1862–1937) and Kate Chopin (1850–1904). To some extent, their individual lives as well as the subjects of their stories reflected the plight of women in those times. It is fitting that these writers chose the short story as their form, since some critics believe that it is often used to challenge social norms.

Gilman was the least gifted of the three as a writer of fiction. She was an economist and an academic whose main contribution to the history of modern short stories is the celebrated 'The Yellow Wallpaper' (1892). The story concerns the mental breakdown of the main female character due to the 'treatment' she receives at the hands of the male characters. The story has endured, perhaps because of its telling images of female entrapment and madness, both of which were powerful metaphors for women's inequality at the time.

Wharton also used the idea of enclosure, although for her it represented a broader concept of 'tradition' than the state of women's lives at the time. Wharton wrote 86 short stories between 1891 and 1937. She tended to write pessimistically about middle class women's lives, although she did not wish to be identified with the women's movement. In both the short stories and the novels (for example, *Ethan Frome*, 1911) there is a conflict between individual fulfilment and the greater needs of society. This conflict reflects the belief of Frank O'Connor, the Irish writer and literary theorist (see Part 4), that the short story speaks for the outsider in society, both with respect to characters in the stories and the writers themselves. Like Henry James (page 28), Wharton felt that she did not belong in America, and like the later Katherine Mansfield, she tended to write of women as failing to overcome their limitations.

Chopin has been 'rediscovered' in recent years, with some of her work first published as late as the 1960s. Although essentially a short story writer, she became known for her novel *The Awakening* (1899), a story that approved of adultery and ended in suicide, thus shocking contemporary reviewers and readers alike. The popular view of what happened concerning this novel is that after the bad reviews Chopin never wrote another word and died a few years later. This account tends to mythologise the misunderstood woman, oppressed by unsympathetic male publishers, but it is only part truth. Chopin published two collections of stories in the 1890s, *Bayou Folk* (1894) and *A Night in Acadie* (1897). The first of these established her as a local colourist – a writer whose stories are set in a real location and which create a picture of the character and lifestyle of the people. The second was less conventional both in its form and content, and confused reviewers. After *The Awakening*, the contract for Chopin's third collection, *A Vocation and a Voice*, was cancelled because her publisher was making cutbacks from his list – no explicit connection was made with *The Awakening*.

Chopin acknowledged the influence of Guy de Maupassant (see page 15) on both her subject matter and style. From Maupassant, she learned objectivity – that is to describe outwardly observable events without commentary. It is partly this feature that makes Chopin sound modern to present-day readers, alongside the fact that many American writers lacked the verbosity that marks a great deal of 19th-century British literature. But it is also Chopin's inclination to write about taboo subjects that sets her apart as a writer ahead of her time, anticipating much of what was to come in the modernist era in the early years of the 20th century.

▶ Gilman's story 'The Yellow Wallpaper' can be read in at least two ways. Do you find it more satisfactory to read it as a protest against 'the rest cure', or as a statement about the position of women in late 19th-century society? Refer to Elaine Showalter's *The Female Malady* (1987) as a starting point.

▶ Chopin's 'The Story of an Hour' can be read in different ways: as a feminist story; as a story in which point of view and reversal of expectation at the end are used to great effect; as a story with biographical and psychological relevance for Chopin. Investigate and compare these three readings of the story.

Loss of certainty: from 19th to 20th century

In the last decade of the 19th century, people in Britain had begun to feel that the old ways were failing and that change was imminent. Britain's economic and naval power no longer went unchallenged. A new role for women in society was beginning to emerge. The great historical event that was the outcome of this changing world, and that did a great deal to change it even further, was the First World War (1914–1918). But there were also literary consequences. Writers such as Oscar Wilde challenged the idea that art had to be associated with moral values, introducing the notion of 'art for art's sake'. It was partly because of ideas like this that short stories were more able to stand on their own. There was less need for stories 'to be worthy of telling' – able to captivate a live audience – or to be attached to a moral, as they often had been in the past. The short story was now ready to stand alone as a 'slice of life'.

The end of the 19th century threatened many of the ideas that had held Victorian society together. These changes can be characterised by a loss of certainty, influencing all kinds of literature, including the short story. Charles Darwin's theory of evolution (1859, 1871) undermined Christian beliefs and the notion that humans are fundamentally different from animals, which many Victorians found shocking. Karl Marx's theories (1867–1895) formed the basis of communism undermining many of the basic economic principles of capitalism. In 1900, Sigmund Freud added the idea of an unconscious mind to the conscious mind and thus called into question individuals' responsibility for their own behaviour. This loss of certainty applied particularly to developments in the field of human psychology which were opening up completely new dimensions for the exploration of human motivation.

These ideas influenced literature in subtle but important ways. Stevenson's *Dr Jekyll and Mr Hyde* and Henry James' 'The Jolly Corner' (1905) both explored the darker side of the unconscious. Plot as a series of linked actions began to be replaced by the drama of the mind, allowing the stories to become more subtle and the action less significant. Joseph Conrad's 'The Secret Sharer' (1912) managed to combine a gripping plot with this new concern for psychology. Many Victorian novels had ended in marriage, but writers such as Thomas Hardy questioned the stability that this implied. Short stories began to see marriage as a starting point (for example, Chekhov's 'Lady with a Lapdog') rather than as a solution, and dealt with different aspects of marriage, including its breakdown. The critic Valery Shaw sees the short story as a form that began to challenge what romantically oriented novels had taken for granted, although novels published towards the end of the 19th century were also beginning to do this. Another sign of society's crumbling confidence was the gradual loss of the **omniscient narrator** – the all-seeing narrator who controlled the whole story, playing god for the reader. Increasingly, characters simply spoke for themselves, making the reader's job of interpretation more demanding. This was particularly the case when the narrator was **unreliable**, as in Henry James' *The Turn of the Screw* (1898).

At the turn of the century, magazine stories were thriving, especially in America, although even in Britain there were more short stories than serialised novels appearing in magazines. These stories catered for a mass audience and therefore began to take on more and more popular appeal, especially in the 'twist in the tale' stories of writers such as O. Henry (1862–1910). Partly because of the influence of modernism (see page 30), the 'popular' story and the **'art' story** separated in the first two decades of the 20th century. However, modern readers would still be shocked to see stories as peculiar as those by Djuna Barnes (1892–1982), published in the New York mainstream press in the 1920s. Barnes' stories, for example, contained metaphors as bizarre as: 'Paprika had a moribund mother under the counterpane, a chaperone who never spoke or moved, since she was paralysed, but who was a pretty good one at that, being a white exclamation point this side of error…' (from 'Paprika Johnson' in *Smoke and Other Early Stories*). But the art story was intended for more than entertainment and would reward serious study: this was the age of modernism and it strongly influenced writing during the rest of the 20th century.

The writers who began to mark the change from a 19th-century style to a 20th-century style were Henry James, the late Rudyard Kipling, Joseph Conrad and James Joyce. The *Yellow Book* was a journal, launched in 1894, that provided a platform for much of this new writing.

▶ Make a survey of the 19th and 20th century stories in Part 3. Tabulate the differences and similarities, perhaps using the following headings: subject matter, vocabulary, narrator, endings.

Henry James

Henry James (1843–1916) wrote novels and short stories between 1875 and his death in 1916. He was therefore writing during a period that saw the end of the Victorian era and the beginning of the First World War. James was best known for his short novels or novellas, such as *The Turn of the Screw* (1898) and *The Ambassadors* (1903), but he also wrote 112 short stories. James was born in America but, like many American writers of the time, spent much of his life living in England, becoming a British subject just before his death. In order fully to understand James as a short story writer, it is necessary to grasp the sense in which he spanned two eras and two continents.

America had been a British colony until 1776. For the first half of the 19th century it had struggled to assert its literary independence, although the short story had certainly helped towards this. In other respects, the literary relationship between the two countries was strained; for example, until the change in copyright laws in the 1890s, the development of American literature had been held back by the cheap reproduction of English literature at the expense of work by American writers. In broader terms, it is also worth remembering that America was still attempting to establish a society in what had been a huge wilderness and that the Western Frontier only ceased to exist in about 1890. By the late 19th century America was catching up, certainly in terms of wealth, but for James it lacked the culture, the history, the civilisation that he saw as a necessary backbone for novel writing. In 1879 he wrote: 'Items of high civilisation missing from American life: a court, an aristocracy, an established church; country houses, cathedrals, old universities and schools; the arts, a political society, a sporting class.' Although James undoubtedly set himself extremely high standards in these matters, the list suggests some of the differences between the two countries at the time.

The 'international theme', which explored the relationship between Americans and the British, became a recurring theme for James. This reflected his own position as an isolated artist, an American who did not feel that he belonged in his own country, and as a writer whose work was largely unappreciated during his lifetime. Interestingly, these ideas fit rather well with O'Connor's theory of the short story (see page 106). 'The Lesson of the Master'(1888), 'The Figure in the Carpet'(1896) and 'The Aspern Papers' (1888) are some of his best known stories about the role of the artist in society. 'The Jolly Corner' is a highly rated story that sums up his personal feelings about America and Britain.

James' wrote during Queen Victoria's reign, and in some respects, wrote with the wordiness of a Victorian – H.G. Wells likened his prose to a 'hippopotamus pushing a pea'. Yet, as a writer of short stories, he anticipated modernism, the literary movement that dominated the first three decades of the 20th century. Here are the factors that make James an important forerunner of modernism:

- He saw story not as sermon or just narrative, but as something much more richly patterned.
- He required a great deal of participation on the part of his readers to piece together his stories.
- He experimented with methods of story telling.
- He gradually phased out the omniscient narrator or authorial voice (see page 27).
- He became more interested in his characters' psychology than in action. Henry's brother William James coined the term **stream of consciousness** to capture the inner life of a person.

Some of James' stories focused on a single idea, just as in Poe's theory of the short story. But here the comparison ends. For Poe, the idea was a situation with intense and sensational possibilities; for James, the idea was usually intellectual. This idea would then be explored from several angles, exhaustingly so, for some readers. In 'The Real Thing' (1893), for example, an artist wants to paint typical aristocrats, but finds that ordinary people are better models than the real thing. The story becomes a comment on the role of the imagination in creating a work of art. Although this intensity of focus was to become more and more the style of short stories in the 20th century, it would also move towards conciseness and suggestion to such an extent that James' work is unfashionable today.

Other 19th-century writers of the short story

The British writer H.H. Munro (1870–1916), who wrote under the pseudonym 'Saki', is known for his somewhat macabre tales that were neatly constructed and frequently ended with a twist. In America, Stephen Crane's notable short stories were, for example, 'The Open Boat' (1897) and 'The Bride Comes to Yellow Sky' (1898). Other short story writers include W.W. Jacobs (1863–1943) who wrote the celebrated 'The Monkey's Paw' (1902); and the Americans Ambrose Bierce who wrote 'An Occurrence at Owl Creek Bridge' (1891), and Bret Harte who wrote 'The Outcasts of Poker Flat' (1870).

Modernism and short stories

Modernism emerged over a period of several years and spread gradually throughout the arts – literature, fine art, the theatre. Elements of modernism were visible in the work of some late 19th-century short story writers such as Rudyard Kipling and Henry James, but it is mainly associated with the first decades of the 20th century.

Modernism was essentially a reaction against the Victorian age. It recognised that the world was not the place of certainties that it had seemed for much of the 19th century. And short story writing was to reflect those changes. Much more attention was paid to the form of a piece of writing. Writers such as Virginia Woolf and Katherine Mansfield began to experiment with unusual ways of telling stories, as style became a new focus of writers' attention. This went hand-in-hand with the new interest in psychology which demanded new means of expression such as 'stream of consciousness'. These new methods varied from writer to writer, but in general there was much less need to tell a story in the traditional sense. Metaphor and symbol were raised to greater prominence; ambiguity became the norm, especially with the loss of the all-seeing, all-knowing narrative voice. If there was an underlying attitude that characterised modernism it was one of alienation – alienation between the people in society and between the artist and society. The characteristic modernist means of expression is summed up by the word 'fragmentation'.

James Joyce and *Dubliners*

'… That supreme but unwanted volume.' (H.E. Bates)

James Joyce (1882–1941) was not a prolific writer of short stories, but the timing and quality of his only collection, *Dubliners* (1914), make it a centrally important text in any history of the short story. *Dubliners* is a set of stories about the lives of ordinary people in Dublin. The collection takes the form of a 'story cycle' in which several stories are set in the same place, they may contain the same characters or be linked by the same theme. *Dubliners* is of particular interest here because issues surrounding its publication are relevant to the kinds of stories that Joyce was writing.

'The Sisters' and 'Eveline' were published individually in 1904 with the other stories being completed for the whole collection by 1907. The final story, 'The Dead', was the last of these. The sequence of the stories follows from childhood to adolescence through to maturity, and the underlying theme is 'paralysis' – the spiritual paralysis of the people of a city, implying powerlessness, frustration, entrapment, and so forth. 'Paralysis' as a theme is well-established amongst critics because of the circumstances of the publication of the book. When Joyce passed the manuscript to his publisher there were objections both from the publisher and from the printer to some of the sexually explicit material (for the time) it contained. In order to resolve these difficulties, Joyce corresponded with the printer, Richards, with the much-quoted words:

> My intention was to write a chapter of the moral history of my country and I chose Dublin for the scene because that city seemed to me the centre of paralysis. I have tried to present it to the indifferent public under four of its aspects: childhood, adolescence, maturity and public life.

But why should Joyce have seen the city and its people in this way? Answers may be found in the political and religious context of Ireland at the turn of the 19th century, when Joyce was writing. Ireland has been split by religion and politics since Protestants settled the north of a Catholic country in the 17th century, creating the divide that dominates even today. Republicans were Irish Catholics who were intent on reunifying the country, but whose cause had suffered by the end of the 19th century. In an attempt to help re-establish an Irish identity many people began to revive Irish folklore and language, but Joyce saw this as a conservative step against the true interests of Ireland. Closely associated with these ideas was the Catholic church which Joyce regarded as narrow in its outlook and a negative force. He would therefore have seen these factors as playing a part in the paralysis.

However, in spite of the apparently overwhelming evidence for the central theme of paralysis, it is possible to argue against it. When Joyce spoke of paralysis, he was trying to convince a publisher for whom he had little respect that he should go ahead with publication. He would have been likely to describe the book in far more conservative terms than was in fact the case. In fact, Joyce suggested that in writing the stories he was merely continuing a 19th-century tradition of writing 'improving literature', from which the reader was expected to learn a moral lesson. But given the style of the stories, this argument is plainly ridiculous: more than ever before, the stories are deliberately ambiguous, requiring large helpings of participation from the reader to complete their meanings.

In this respect, Anthony Burgess wrote in 1973:

> ... few people were ready for it: the taste was for didacticism, the pedestrian moral lessons of a less naturalistic fiction. In *Dubliners* the reader was not told what to think about the characters and their actions, or rather inactions. There were no great sins, nor any performance of great good.

For example, in 'Clay' the pathetic, isolated Maria is tricked into putting her hand into wet clay, but the reader is told only that Maria scarcely even notices what has happened. Neither is the substance itself named – the reader is left to infer that it is clay from the title of the story. The events that follow are all bare facts and provide Maria's limited perception of the situation. Maria's song, 'I dreamt I dwelt in marble halls' and the clay itself probably symbolise her hopes and the grim reality of imminent death. Readers are left to weave together all of these factors in a narrative that merely appears mundane. By contrast, Joyce's later novels worked by embellishing, by building up multiple layers of meaning instead of leaving things out. It is easy therefore to overlook the spareness that makes *Dubliners* so important, but it made way for more extreme versions of the same technique, for example, in the work of Ernest Hemingway (see page 34).

Arguably, Joyce is also a key figure in short story history because, like Poe, he contributed a central idea to short story theory. The term **epiphany** was originally a biblical word meaning 'showing' and referred to the showing of the baby Jesus to the three kings in the nativity story. Joyce, who liked to intellectualise using religious terminology, adopted the term to refer to an illuminating moment at the heart of a story. Such a moment occurs in 'An Encounter' in which the boy narrator experiences a child abuser, and it is this encounter that leads him to say of his friend Mahoney that 'in my heart I had always despised him a little'. Thus the epiphany has changed the character in a subtle but significant way. Joyce, in developing epiphany in short stories was building on a notebook of epiphanies – mundane but significant experiences in his own life – that he had kept as a young man. The term has been used to describe the purpose of short stories published since *Dubliners*. It is dealt with in more detail in Part 4.

Virginia Woolf

Virginia Woolf (1882–1941) is best known for her modernist novels such as *Mrs Dalloway* (1925) and *To the Lighthouse* (1927). Woolf was one of the central members of the Bloomsbury group, some half dozen writers devoted to aesthetic appreciation and artistic revolt against the restrictions of Victorian society. She was considered by many to be the weakest of the modernist writers until her reputation was enhanced by feminist critics from the 1960s.

Which contextual factors need to be considered in connection with Virginia Woolf?

- Gender: towards the end of the 19th century, women had begun writing about women's role in society and in 1928 women gained full suffrage in Britain. Woolf frequently wrote about expectations of and roles played by men and women.

- Short story plots up to this time: with the notable exception of Chekhov (see page 16), 19th-century short stories had been dominated by strong plots and climactic endings. Woolf consciously set out to challenge these narrative conventions which she saw as male creations.

- Woolf began writing at the end of the Victorian era when there were new ways of thinking about art, society and psychology. She was particularly concerned to capture the psychology of the present moment in her stories.

Virginia Woolf's short stories made an enormous contribution to the development of the form. Instead of being dominated by what had gone before in the work of established male writers such as H.G. Wells (1866–1946) and Arnold Bennett (1867–1931), she wanted to capture in writing human consciousness or experience as directly as possible. In her own words she set out to capture 'an ordinary mind on an ordinary day', although many critics felt more comfortable with the 'ordinariness' of Wells and Bennett. Like a lot of writing after the First World War, her work bore an air of disillusion and an unwillingness to indulge the reader in romance or adventure.

'Kew Gardens' (1919) was to become a perfect example of one particular type of modernist story. It has no plot development in the conventional sense and depends for its meaning on patterns of ideas and images. Such a story can be contrasted in terms of plot with the traditional tale in which a series of connected events lead to a conclusive ending. Woolf's stories were as plotless as those of Chekhov, but much more experimental. In stories like 'The Haunted House' (1921), for example, it is difficult to untangle the real from the unreal. But her experiments went further than this. She even set out to disrupt the normal hierarchy of characters and scenes in fictional writing; in conventional stories, objects and scenes are there to say something about the human world and are therefore subservient to it. But Woolf wanted objects to be simply themselves, not stand for anything else. She also saw herself as breaking down barriers between different kinds of writing – stories, letters, diaries – and indeed her work often reads like poetry. In this respect, she was influenced by the sketch writers of 50 years before such as Thomas De Quincy (1785–1859). As a modernist she was the opposite of Hemingway: she was experimental, difficult, psychological; he was mundane, apparently superficial, deceptively easy.

Ernest Hemingway

'Get the most out of the least,' said Ernest Hemingway (1899–1961). More than any other writer, perhaps before or since, he pared down his style to the bare minimum so that, rather like an iceberg, most of the substance in Hemingway's stories lies beneath the surface. This tendency towards surface simplicity and the value placed on minimalism in story telling in the late 20th century made Hemingway probably the single most influential short story writer in English of the last hundred years.

Whilst working as a journalist, Hemingway became one of many American writers drawn to the flourishing literary and artistic atmosphere of Paris in the 1920s. Paris was at the centre of innovative movements such as Cubism and Surrealism in the field of fine art, and of modernism in the literary world:

> … if you were a young unpublished writer with radical ambitions, like Ernest Hemingway, who arrived in December 1921, Paris was the only place to be. It was the centre of experiment, the creative writing class of the twenties, the university of Modernism…Year after year, writers swarmed in from everywhere, driven by exile, post-war political upheaval, literary censorship, or just the need for a drink. London had grown depressed after the war. The United States had President Harding, Puritanism and Prohibition.
>
> (Malcolm Bradbury, ed. *The Atlas of Literature*, 1996)

These exiled writers became known as 'The Lost Generation' whose predominant mood after the First World War was one of disillusion. This mood reflected much of the writing of this period, such as T.S. Eliot's poem *The Waste Land* (1922).

Hemingway's novels such as *A Farewell to Arms* (1929) made him famous with the general public, but his short stories were more extreme in their experiments with style. His best known collections of stories are *In Our Time* (1925) and *Men Without Women* (1927) which many regard as greater achievements than his novels. His macho attitude and interest in big game hunting made him easy prey for feminist critics in later years.

His short stories often did away with plot to such an extent that they seemed to be an advertisement for Chekhov's comment about writing the story and then deleting the beginning and the end. The result was fragments that gave the reader a great deal to do and made Hemingway a pioneer of the short short story (see page 52). So, for example, stories such as 'Hills Like White Elephants' (1927) and 'The End of Something' (1925) seem like little more than aimless fragments of conversation that qualify as stories only with the reader's considerable imaginative input. Hemingway is often frustratingly simple, even banal; Wyndham Lewis's term for Hemingway's inarticulate hero was 'dumb ox':

'What's yours?' George asked them.
'I don't know,' one of the men said. 'What do you want to eat, Al?'
'I don't know,' said Al. 'I don't know what I want to eat.'

('The Killers', 1927)

Hemingway's style was another variant on the modernist theme, but it met with varying reactions. Frank O'Connor, the Irish writer and literary theorist (see Part 4), felt that Hemingway simply didn't give the reader enough information. In contrast Nadine Gordimer, a late 20th-century writer (see page 43), has claimed that everyone who was writing short stories in the 1940s was influenced by him. Even more than Maupassant, Hemingway wrote objectively – describing only what he saw on the outside. Adjectives and descriptions of emotions or feelings rarely appeared, so that the stoicism of his style seemed to match his theme. There is sometimes an epiphany, sometimes a failed epiphany and sometimes just an atmosphere or state of mind that arises from a situation. Repetition of ordinary words is a prominent feature of Hemingway's stories and although this may seem at times like mere carelessness, David Lodge (*The Art of Fiction*, 1992) has shown that this works to subtle effect. This casualness in Hemingway's style is deceptive because, like another layer beneath the surface, he constructs a complex pattern of images, rhythms and symbols. Lodge provides useful alternative readings of 'Cat in the Rain' (1927), illustrating well this underlying complexity (*Working with Structuralism*, 1981).

In a number of senses, short stories had moved away from the sensational and the spectacular in the first 100 years or so of their existence. In the 19th century Poe's stories had been bizarre, Hardy's were about unusual incidents that had to be worth the telling, even Henry James wrote ghost stories, although he also tackled abstract issues – like the cultural differences between England and America and the nature of art. By the early 20th century, Katherine Mansfield and Hemingway were writing about the ordinary in an apparently ordinary way, and Hemingway, in particular, took this style to extremes, stripping the short story of the elegance associated with a writer such as Henry James. It was fitting that an American should have done this: American writing had for a long time been less ornate than English, more down to earth, more in tune with the rhythms of daily speech. Hemingway, like other modernists but even more so, trimmed away explanation and comment. These features were permanently excluded after Hemingway – and the short story has never looked back.

D.H. Lawrence

D.H. Lawrence (1885–1930) was no innovator when it came to short stories. He was best known for novels such as *Sons and Lovers* (1913), *The Rainbow* (1915) and *Women in Love* (1920). These novels explored Lawrence's radical ideas about human relationships and sexuality which were influenced by the psychoanalyst Sigmund Freud. More than ever before, Lawrence's stories explored the idea that people's motives for their actions were unconscious and deeply linked to sexuality and work. He wrote over 70 short stories, most of which were conventional in structure compared with the experiments of writers such as Woolf and Mansfield.

Lawrence's explicit treatment of sexuality meant that he anticipated the more liberal attitudes that were to emerge much later in the 20th century, especially in the 1960s. Like his novels, Lawrence's short stories drew attention for their content rather than their form, although like his contemporaries he tended towards unresolved plots and he was a modernist in so far as he relied heavily on the use of symbols in his stories. Unlike most modernists he seemed to care little about form, believing that an appropriate way of writing would simply emerge from the emotion. He published three collections of short stories during his lifetime: *The Prussian Officer* (1914), *England, My England* (1914) and *The Woman Who Rode Away* (1922).

The First World War played a major part in Lawrence's development as a writer. Before the war Lawrence had preached for women to be taken seriously, for men to take on board something of the way that women see the world. But during the war women took over many of the jobs that had traditionally been done by men, such as factory workers or bus conductors. This, however, was not what Lawrence had wanted. He came to adopt an anti-feminist stance that asserted male supremacy over women and what they had become because of the war. This view is expressed most explicitly in 'Tickets Please!', 'Monkey Nuts', and 'The Fox', all of which were written within six months of the end of the war.

H.E. Bates regarded D.H. Lawrence's short stories as his best achievement:

> … his stories are always an expression of a more direct, more controlled and more objective art. In them Lawrence has no time to preach, to lose his temper, to go mystical, or to persuade the reader to listen to him by the doubtful process of shouting at the top of his voice and finally kicking him downstairs. Lawrence is for once bound to say what he has to say within reasonable, and even strict, limits of time and space. Ordinarily dictatorial, Lawrence is here dictated to by the form he has chosen. The results have little of that slobbering hysteria of the later novels; they are again and again a superb expression of Lawrence's greatest natural gifts, sensibility, vision, a

supreme sense of the physical (whether beautiful or ugly, human or otherwise), an uncanny sense of place, and a flaming vitality. Unobscured by hysteria, by the passion of theoretical gospels, these qualities shine through three-quarters of the forty stories that Lawrence wrote .... Later generations will react to the novels of Lawrence much as we now react to the novels of Hardy. The philosophical rumblings will date; the wonderful pictures, the life directly projected, will remain. From such a test the short stories will emerge as the more durable achievement.

(H.E. Bates The Modern Short Story, 1941)

▶ Read the extract from the end of 'Tickets Please!' (Part 3, pages 81–83). Then read Hilary Simpson's comments on the story below. Do you interpret Simpson's position as feminist or anti-feminist? How do you interpret the story yourself?

The feeling that prevails at the end of the story is that something stupendous has happened, that things have got out of hand, that the women have gone further than they intended. By bonding together to humiliate the promiscuous male, the women have indeed broken several taboos of patriarchy, and their sense of the enormity of what they have done is justified. They have attacked the double standard and their own status as sexual objects; attacked the notion that women are incapable of solidarity and must always compete with each other when a man is at stake; and shown themselves capable of violent action. It is partly because of this breaking of taboos that the story has a powerful and shocking quality. It is also Lawrence at his technical best, the build-up of tension as friendly revenge turns to actual physical assault being particularly well-handled; and the various elements – realism, symbolism, mythology, psychological observation – are painlessly integrated.

(Hilary Simpson *D.H. Lawrence* in *Longman Critical Readers*, 1987)

Katherine Mansfield

Katherine Mansfield (1888–1923) is one of the few 20th-century writers to make her reputation solely by writing short stories, although had she lived longer she might have gone on to produce novels. She wrote 88 stories and published three collections during her lifetime: *In a German Pension* (1911), *Bliss and other Stories* (1920) and *The Garden Party and other Stories* (1922). She attempted to write novels, but none of these attempts was successful. She died of consumption at the age of 34. Like Virginia Woolf, she is regarded as one of the first modernist writers.

Mansfield did not start writing her best stories until after the First World War and came to regard her first collection as sub-standard. Like Virginia Woolf she wrote about ordinary lives – life's 'tremendous trifles' – and linked her determination to develop a new style of short story with the First World War: 'I feel the profoundest sense that nothing can ever be the same – that as artists we are traitors if we feel otherwise; we have to take it into account and find new expressions, new moulds for our thoughts and feelings.' (quoted in Gillian Boddy *Katherine Mansfield: The Woman and the Writer*, 1988) Some saw her stories as fragments or sketches because plot was less important than character and mood; in this respect she resembled Chekhov, who was one of her greatest influences. Her method of telling stories was often casual and oblique in that it seemed to approach the story telling indirectly, apparently just letting information drift out to the reader instead of ordering events according to a logical pattern. Like James Joyce and other modernists, what she left out was very important.

Many of the early stories were about aloneness and isolation and, as an exile from New Zealand living in Europe, Mansfield seemed to be writing her own life in these stories. They are sometimes accused of being sentimental accounts from the lives of lonely old women, as in the case of 'The Life of Ma Parker' (1922). But Mansfield followed Chekhov in trying to eliminate the personal from her writing. So in later work, she avoided the sentimental by presenting her characters ironically. That is, the stories were narrated from the characters' own point of view, but they were incapable of seeing themselves in the way that readers could. In 'The Daughters of the Late Colonel' (1922), Mansfield reveals the indecision of two middle-aged women whose lives were dominated by their now dead father. Here, her narrative technique is innovatory in that past and present unfold at the same time, the past through the consciousness of the two leading characters. But many readers have mistaken her intention to reveal 'the hidden beauty' in these women's lives for cruelty, as if Mansfield was making fun of the two women. This demonstrates one of the problems of interpreting modernist fiction – that of judging the author's attitude to her subject when it is left to speak for itself.

The later stories, especially 'Prelude' (1918) and 'At the Bay' (1922), when she seems to regain touch with her childhood, are generally regarded as her best work. The former, a story about the end of a girl's childhood, Mansfield had intended to be a novel. Like 'The Daughters of the Late Colonel', 'Prelude' takes an unusual form in that it is divided into 12 episodes, not necessarily following on from each other chronologically like chapters, but each unfolding a different aspect of the central idea of the story. 'Prelude' was her most innovative story, using multiple voices rather than a narrator to create its characters. These innovations are testimony to Mansfield's constant determination to perfect every word so that her work was, according to the critic C.K.Stead, '… at every point authentic, a recreation of life, so that we experience and remember actual life itself'.

James Joyce's notion of epiphany is useful for assessing Mansfield's work. Mansfield has been both praised and criticised for her treatment of epiphanies (see pages 105 and 111). H.E. Bates, for example, thinks she was not an originator. She did not 'disrupt the prose of her time as Joyce did'. The contemporary critic, Dominic Head, on the other hand, believes that the disruption of narrative conventions was an important part of her style, and that this extended as far as epiphanies. Head argues that the idea of epiphany could be seen as simplistic – if considered as a simple revelatory moment when characters learn something significant about themselves. Realising this, Mansfield seemed to undermine her own epiphanies by complicating them with competing emotions, much as in real life. 'Bliss' (1920) is a good story for exploring this idea. Some feminist critics have found her disappointing with respect to epiphanies as 'the moment of self-awareness is also the moment of self-betrayal' (Elaine Showalter *A Literature of Their Own: British Women Novelists from Brontë to Lessing*, 1988).

William Faulkner

> Rarely has a great short story writer started out with such low sights. Without monetary need, it is very possible Faulkner would not have shaped himself to the short story market, but, instead, remained with longer fiction …
>
> (Frederick Karl *William Faulkner: American Writer*, 1989)

William Faulkner (1897–1962) was an American modernist who created in his novels and short stories a vast imaginary county in the southern states of America: Yoknapatawpha. He is best known for novels such as *The Sound and the Fury* (1929) and *As I Lay Dying* (1930), but he also wrote several collections of short stories. The short stories tend to be less experimental, but the novels often used stream of consciousness writing, such as when Faulkner represents the thoughts of Benjy, the idiot in *The Sound and the Fury*. His work was not fully recognised until after the Second World War when he won the Nobel Prize in 1949.

Faulkner's views on the writing of short stories are vivid. He called it 'going whoring' because it was a quick way of making money in between novels. Faulkner is a classic case of a writer whose output was influenced by commercial pressures although he held out against the demands of many magazine publishers. For much of his career he was forced to write commercial stories for mass circulation magazines such as *Saturday Evening Post*. By complete contrast, and almost in contradiction, he said that writing short stories was much more exacting than writing novels because in a novel you could be more careless. In a short story almost every word had to be almost exactly right.

One of Faulkner's most prominent themes was the decay of the American South from the time of the Civil War in the 1860s. This war had been about slavery – the South wanted to maintain slavery because it was economically dependent on it, whereas the North was not. After the South lost the war there followed a period of depression in the southern states. Faulkner dramatised this in his stories, peeling away the surface to reveal corruption and decay, although some critics feel that he caricatured the South with images of incest, sadism and necrophilia for sensational effect, a style sometimes referred to as 'southern gothic'. Certainly, Faulkner lived at a time when the South was changing from a place associated with racism, classism, violence and agriculture to a modern, industrial suburban community. This allowed him to create his complex web of stories and novels, but some have argued that it is often difficult to tell if he was on the side of the aristocrat, the negro or the Indian.

Faulkner frequently used the device of a narrator who is a character in the story. Sometimes his stories resemble yarns and, in a manner similar at times to Kipling, he creates the situation of a group of men listening to a story teller and frequently interrupting him, so that there is an interaction between the moment of telling and the story told, as in the early story 'The Liar' (1925). Often, time is not treated in a linear fashion, as in 'A Rose for Emily' (1931). In other stories the action circles around a central event that the reader never sees, as in 'Dry September' (1931). 'The Bear' (1942), one of his best known stories, famously includes a very long sentence to represent the consciousness of one his characters. In these ways, Faulkner marked himself out as a modernist but not an innovatory writer of short stories.

For some critics *Go Down Moses and Other Stories* (1942) was a landmark volume in Faulkner's career, although the reviews it received were not generally favourable. Right from the start Faulkner had been influenced by Sherwood Anderson and in creating a series of linked stories he was following in the tradition of short story cycle writers. The problem with the collection was that at times passages were obscure, but it was probably rated highly because, in contrast to the unevenness of Faulkner's earlier collections, the links meant that the reader had to think beyond the individual stories.

Other writers of the modernist era

These include Joseph Conrad (1857–1924) who wrote 'An Outpost of Progress' (1898), and A.E. Coppard (1878-1957) whose collection *The Black Dog* (1923) is rated as amongst his best.

Writers of 1930s, 1940s and 1950s

This period can be seen as a still passage between two innovatory times – modernism and post-modernism. In all forms of literature, the period is known for its conservatism. The formal experiments of modernism were dismissed as élitist and many writers concerned themselves with social issues for which the appropriate form was realism. The depression of the 1930s and the Second World War, for example, gave writers new experiences to write about, and in the post-war years much fictional writing focused on social class. Some critics have claimed that, particularly in the immediate post-war years, there was no new direction in which the short story could go and that the form was in decline. However, this lack of experiment does not mean that the period was insignificant. It in fact produced several great short story writers, many of whom continued to work well into the post-modernist period which began in the 1960s.

In Britain, V.S. Pritchett (1900–1997) captured the English middle and working classes with shrewd observation in stories such as 'The Camberwell Beauty' (1974). Elizabeth Bowen (1899–1973) who was influenced by Henry James, wrote social comedy and stories about the war but not 'war stories', notably 'Mysterious Kor' (1944). In America, Eudora Welty tapped into modernist thinking and the southern gothic begun by Faulkner. Welty wrote, for example, of the struggle of individuals to uphold their values against the power of the southern family. 'Clytie' (1941) is a gothic story that uses images of female entrapment leading to death, much in the same style as Charlotte Perkins Gilman's 'The Yellow Wallpaper'. Somerset Maugham (1874-1965) was a versatile writer in many forms who achieved great popularity in his long career. His several volumes of short stories showed him to be a conservative writer of short stories, often imitating an oral style and with the inevitable final twist. In spite of his somewhat second rate reputation, some of his stories are amongst the best in English.

Other writers of the period include: Katherine Anne Porter (1890–1980), with her collection of short stories *Pale Horse, Pale Rider* (1939); Frank O'Connor (1903–1966), many of whose stories capture childhood in Ireland in the mid-20th century; Flannery O'Connor (1925–1964), a southern gothic writer whose *Complete Short Stories* was published in 1971; H.E. Bates (1905–1974) who produced a prolific number of stories centring on English rural life.

Contemporary and post-modern short stories

The 1960s began a period of prosperity in the Western world that led to a questioning of many of society's values and the setting up of 'alternative cultures'. There was a new surge in the women's movement, granting women greater sexual freedom, and there was renewed vigour in movements promoting racial equality. Western cultures began to listen to the many ethnic voices that were producing literature from within their midst. Short story writers questioned traditional methods in a way that was far more radical than the modernist movement. Arguably, if the short story had gained from modernism, it positively shone under the influence of post-modernism.

Most critics see the short story as dividing into a variety of sub-genres after the Second World War. They argue that the following forms developed: **magic realism** which draws on fantasy, myth and fairy tale; experiment, which breaks the rules, plays with language and focuses on the bizarre; realism, which continues to develop the early 20th-century form; self-conscious fiction which draws attention to itself as fiction and is sometimes called **metafiction**. If there is a special kind of short story written by women and by writers from post-colonial cultures, then there may be more sub-genres. Certainly, it becomes increasingly difficult to talk of a single tradition of the short story. Whilst this may be true, one might argue that the short story has always existed in a variety of forms, as is evident throughout this book: plotless and plotted stories; the gothic genre; the significant moment or epiphany; the local colour story and so forth.

Post-modern stories

The name is often more frightening than the idea, which, once understood, is straightforward. Nevertheless, post-modern short stories can be irritating and clearly not designed for a comfortable bedtime read. A good starting point with accessible texts is Margaret Atwood's collection *Good Bones* (1993).

First and foremost, post-modernist texts set out to break the rules. Conventional realism (such as most 19th-century fiction) sets out to project the reader into an imaginary world which is then interpreted according to the arrangement of themes throughout the story. Post-modernism quite deliberately defies these expectations by:

- providing more than one ending
- contradicting itself
- describing things that couldn't possibly happen

- extending a metaphor to the point of absurdity
- blurring the distinction between the imagined world and the reader's real world
- being unresolved at the end.

This type of writing became popular in South America under the influence of writers such as Jorge Luis Borges (1899–1986), reaching, to a lesser extent, the Caribbean. But it also became popular in America with the writing of Donald Barthelme (1931–1989), John Barth, William Gass and Robert Coover. One of Coover's best known stories, 'The Baby Sitter' (1969), provides several versions of the action throughout the story. One branch of post-modernism led to 'anti-stories' which defy attempts to tell a story in the conventional manner. An accessible example is Donald Barthelme's 'Some of us have been threatening our friend Colby' (*Collected Stories*, 1988).

This kind of writing is experimental and therefore extreme, but its influence can be found in much modern writing. For example, today stories are difficult to interpret because ambiguities are built in. It is important to remember that post-modern fiction is about the process of writing fiction and the process of reading, so that the whole business of making sense of the stories is often more important than the subject matter itself. It helps if you see post-modernist short stories as 'playful' and your task is to work out what they are playing with. This idea applies particularly well to Atwood's *Good Bones*.

Although post-modernism was the dominant movement of the last half of the 20th century, not all writers of the period can be called post-modernist. Most writers cannot be identified with a single school of thought because their writing stems from a multitude of influences: social, personal, political, literary.

Nadine Gordimer

Nadine Gordimer is a prolific writer of novels and short stories who has lived all of her life in South Africa. She began writing in the late 1940s and continues to write today. As a result, her work spans the post-war years and the post-modern age. It is interesting therefore to observe the influences of post-modernism on an established writer. Much of Gordimer's work is about the plight of blacks living under the apartheid regime in South Africa that treated them as second class citizens until it was abolished in 1991. Her work shows a strong sympathy for the black majority of South Africa and, like many short story writers, her other themes are loneliness and isolation. The difference with Gordimer is that these familiar themes are usually given a racial slant.

The apartheid regime began in 1948 when various non-white people were denied full citizenship; for example, non-whites were not allowed to vote even though they outnumbered the whites by at least five to one. The 1950s saw a time of optimism for movements that opposed apartheid within South Africa; there was a flowering of activity among political activists and writers. It was in this context that Gordimer began writing, with her first collection of stories *Face to Face* (1949). This optimism effectively disappeared in 1960 when the police massacred 70 people in a demonstration at Sharpeville. Although many of her contemporaries left at this time, Gordimer stayed in South Africa.

She has written ten collections of short stories, including *Face to Face* (1949), *Six Feet of the Country* (1956) *Friday's Footprint and Other Stories* (1960), *Not for Publication* (1965), *Livingstone's Companions* (1971), *A Soldier's Embrace* (1980) and *Jump* (1991). These stories have reflected the changes in South African society over a 40-year period and they have slowly taken on some of the influences of post-modern style (see page 42). Her earlier stories recount significant moments in people's lives in the context of apartheid South Africa. For example, 'Is There Nowhere Else Where We Can Meet?' (1951) is a straightforward narrative from the point of view of a white woman who is attacked by a 'native' (in later stories this word is replaced by 'African' and 'black'). The woman undergoes an epiphany in which she realises the futility of fighting the system; she is left with a sense of powerlessness although it is clear that the system is not hers. Forty years later 'Once Upon a Time' (see Part 3, pages 94–98) is altogether more playful in its style and the situation of white liberals is much more extreme, more desperate. This time it is not just a chance encounter that provides the significant moment, but it is the whole of the white South African way of life under apartheid that is undermined.

Much of Gordimer's work has been about the impotence of white middle class liberalism under the apartheid regime. In other words, she sees the moderate approach to a bad situation as inadequate. The short story form in particular has allowed her to sample the situations of individuals who represent the whole community. As a woman writer who frequently uses female characters and who is obviously 'on the side of women' the question of feminism has often been raised. However, Gordimer has always resisted being classed as a feminist, and in 1988 rejected her candidacy for the Orange Award (an important literary prize) on the grounds that it was restricted to women writers. Gordimer used to insist that 'there is no sex in the brain' but has become less dogmatic about this.

The progress of her work has been summed up like this:

Her focus is on the white community, a society which has welcomed a very high level of material comfort – and pays a heavy price for it with repressive legislation and social strictures. The result has been heightening tension as the individual struggle to hold on to moral values in a world where true feeling and expression are increasingly subdued. Her picture of a society backing into a blind alley is uncompromising and grows bleaker with the years.

(Michael Stapleton *The Cambridge Encyclopedia of Literature*, 1983)

▶ To what extent do you feel that the above statement helps you to read 'Once Upon a Time' on pages 94–98?

Raymond Carver

... it is the ordinary moment which illuminates the most extraordinary things.

(Tess Gallagher Introduction to Raymond Carver
A New Path to the Waterfall, 1989)

Raymond Carver's (1939–1988) work seems to epitomise the contemporary short story. His stories are often depressing and peculiar sketches of life in the modern city. Plot is minimal, so it is not surprising that Carver acknowledged his debt to Chekhov. There is a strong sense of alienation in his presentation of characters and much of this 'dis-ease' reflects the depressing circumstances of his own life. When asked why he wrote short stories, Carver claimed that it was all he had time for, he was often drunk and trying to escape his children who were sending him mad.

Carver's work is perhaps most indebted to Hemingway. The surface of Carver's stories is extremely simple, his grammar and vocabulary colloquial, almost flat and the very opposite of the style of Henry James. John Gardner, Carver's teacher, told him: 'Read all the Faulkner you can get your hands on, and then read all of Hemingway to clean the Faulkner out of your system.' Like Hemingway, Carver is also regarded as a masculine writer in the sense that his own background was tough and there are few stories in which drinking and smoking do not feature. The spareness of Carver's style also contributes to this impression: you are unlikely to find lengthy descriptive passages in his work and his vocabulary is mundane and repetitive. Carver frequently reduced his stories down to the 'marrow', following in the Chekhovian tradition of omission. However, there are a few stories that he expanded and rewrote, like 'The Bath' (1981) which became 'A Small Good Thing' (1983) in the rewritten version.

Carver's collections include *Put Yourself in my Shoes* (1974), *Will You Please Be Quiet, Please* (1976), *Furious Seasons* (1977), *What We Talk about when We Talk About Love* (1981) and *Cathedral* (1983). His early work contained devices like flashbacks and stream of consciousness writing, influenced by Faulkner and Joyce. Later stories were longer, more complex psychologically and, some believe, less pessimistic: 'The stories of *Cathedral* display a new mellowness; the controlled use of epiphanies absent from his earlier fictions emphasises his belief in the ultimate triumph of good over evil.' (Jenny Stringer *The Oxford Companion to 20th Century Literature in English*, 1996) This certainly applies to the beauty of the endings of the title story and 'A Small Good Thing'. But some epiphanies are extremely attenuated, seeming to offer only a glimmer of satisfaction in a disastrous situation, such as when 'Chef's House' ends with 'We still had some fish in the icebox. There wasn't much else. We'll clean it up tonight, I thought, and that will be the end of it.' – the end of the fish but also the end of drying out from alcoholism and the rejuvenated relationship.

The reader gets the impression with Carver's stories that much of the power lies in the contrast between the reader's expectations and what actually happens. Often there is a intense focus on the minutiae of everyday life, giving the impression that something significant is about to happen, but it doesn't. Carver has said: 'There has to be something at stake, something important working itself out from sentence to sentence.' The reader expects a significant ending, perhaps a twist or an epiphany, but often the characters remain trapped in their situation, which is as much psychological as physical. Unlike Hemingway, Carver uses the bizarre alongside the mundane, perhaps influenced by magic realism, such as when a man puts all of his furniture out on the front drive of his house ('Why Don't You Dance', 1981) or when a couple sit down and enjoy eating bread with a man who has given them nuisance calls in connection with the death of their son ('A Small Good Thing', 1983). In this way, Carver creates a black humour.

Carver's stories are severely limited in terms of time and place, and his characters are merely figures in an urban landscape: the unemployed ('Preservation', 1983), alcoholics ('Chef's House'), nameless people living in conflict-ridden suburbia ('One More Thing', 1981; 'Popular Mechanics', 1981). But an additional dimension is added by means of **intertextual** references to such things as the story of King Solomon ('Popular Mechanics' is deeply ironic because of this reference – see page 66), or to the body preserved in a peat bog for thousands of years. Although it can be argued that epiphany is rare in Carver's work, the expectation of an epiphany in the reader can be useful in leading to an interpretation of stories that sometimes seem impenetrable. This means that the reader stops reading for the plot (which will always disappoint in Carver's case) and starts looking for patterns of similarity in the text. 'Preservation', for example (see the extract in Part 3, pages 91–92), is about a man who has just been made redundant and for the first few pages of the story he does little more than lie on the sofa at home. But then Carver builds a pattern relating to the idea of preservation: the body preserved in peat; a man who stays in bed because he is afraid of growing old; the fridge breaking down and ruining the contents; the wife going to an auction to buy a new one. Mysteriously, water appears as the man refuses to eat the food from the fridge. The reader is left wondering if the water symbolises a kind of rebirth, a thawing out because this crisis has drawn him off the sofa. Or the opposite: the man's returning to the sofa at the end is a negative act of self-preservation and the story a grim portrait of the effects of unemployment.

▶ Here are two contrasting views of Carver's work:

> **1** Carver himself felt that he wanted his readers to be 'moved, and maybe even a little haunted'.
> (Tess Gallagher, quoted in Foreword to *No Heroics Please*, 1991)

> **2** In Carver's collection of stories 'What We Talk About When We Talk About Love', language is used so sparingly and plots are so minimal that the stories seem pallidly drained patterns with no flesh and life in them. The stories are so short and lean that they seem to have plot only as we reconstruct them in our memory. Whatever theme they may have is embodied in the bare outlines of the event and in the spare dialogue of characters who are so overcome by event and so lacking in language that the theme is unsayable. Characters often have no names or only first names and are so briefly described that they seem to have no physical presence at all; certainly they have no distinct identity but rather seem to be shadowy presences trapped in their own inarticulateness. The charge against Carver is the same one once lodged against Chekhov, that his fiction is dehumanised and therefore cold and unfeeling.
> (Charles May *The New Short Story Theories*, 1994)

Which of these views best reflects your own reading of Carver? (There is an extract from 'Preservation' in Part 3, pages 91–92.)

Post-colonial short stories

Post-colonial literature comes from Britain's former colonies in the Caribbean, Africa and India, but not usually Canada and Australia because in these countries literature is dominated by descendants of white Europeans. Many post-colonial writers write in English and so their work has come to form an established branch of English literature. The large output of literature in these countries was fuelled in the 20th century by the drive towards independence and, in the Caribbean, by emigration. The short story form often allows a combination of the personal and the political, which most post-colonial writing cannot avoid.

The rise of Caribbean literature coincided with the emergence of short stories at the beginning of the 20th century, although before the Second World War many Caribbean stories were imitations of the tale (see page 11), borrowed from the colonists. It was not until the independence period after the Second World War that writers began to use dialect in stories that came to represent the social and psychological costs of emigration. Writers such as George Lamming, Samuel Selvon (1923–1994) and V.S. Naipaul wrote in a style similar to the realism popular in Britain at the time. Andrew Salkey (1928–1995) and others also drew on their own traditional folk tales, such as the Anancy tales, to express their nationalism, and in this way these stories were influenced by magic realism (see page 42). These writers felt that in order to establish their own identity as a nation it was important to reclaim their myths as their own.

The large output by these writers established the common themes of emigration, home, questions of allegiance, childhood, etc. – all of which are ripe for exploitation within the short story genre. However, Naipaul's case is interesting because he is descended from the Indian migrant workers who were used to replace slaves after abolition. He could therefore be seen as an outsider in a double sense, both in Trinidad and in Britain. This alienation is expressed in stories such as 'The Night Watchman's Occurrence Book' (1969) and in the stories of *Miguel Street* (1959). In recent years, a new generation has often taken an experimental approach, using, for example, magic realism, particularly Jamaica Kincaid, an Antiguan based in America and known for her feminist and strongly anti-British views. The beginning of her story 'My Mother' can be found in Part 3, page 72, Extract 6.

In India there was a strong tradition of writing in English throughout the 20th century, as, for example, in the work of R.K. Narayan and Salman Rushdie, although the latter is more famous as a novelist. Narayan has frequently been compared with Chekhov and Mansfield and has written many volumes, including *Malgudi Days* (1982). Malgudi is a fictional Indian town that features in many of Narayan's stories and novels, in much the same way as Yoknapatawpha worked for Faulkner. A frequent theme of Narayan's, as with many post-colonial writers, is the clash between tradition and Western attitudes. Narayan writes using epiphanies to suggest that his characters, from various walks of Indian life, will emerge from conflict with a new way of seeing the world. However, as with many contemporary short story writers, these aspirations are often not met with success.

Linguistically, post-colonial writing adds another dimension in that the language used to write the story itself becomes a political statement. There is an ongoing debate about the merits of writing in the 'native' language (for example, Hindi, Creole, Yoruba). The choice of writing in English can be seen as allowing the former colonial power to call the tune, and as a rejection of local values. Even within stories written in English, choice of language to represent characters is significant. Often there is an interplay between Standard English and some form of dialect, as for example, in Selvon's 'The Cricket Match' (1957). Sometimes, the entire story is narrated in dialect, as in Geoffrey Philps' 'My Brother's Keeper' (1997).

Other post-colonial short story writers from the Caribbean include Jan Carew (Guyana); Olive Senior (Jamaica); Merle Collins (Grenada); Alecia McKenzie (Jamaica); and from India, Anita Desai whose collections of short stories include *Games at Twilight* (1978) and *Diamond Dust* (2000).

Alice Munro

Alice Munro is a major voice in contemporary short story writing, possibly the greatest living exponent of the form. Her stories are set in rural Canada where she was born and where she lives, and they are often about ordinary lives with disturbing undercurrents. Her reputation rests almost entirely on the several volumes of short stories she has written, including: *Dance of the Happy Shades* (1968), *Something I've Been Meaning to Tell You* (1974), *The Moons of Jupiter* (1982), *Open Secrets* (1994) and *The Love of a Good Woman* (1998). *Lives of Girls and Women* (1971) was an episodic novel. She was shortlisted for the Booker Prize in 1979 for *The Beggar Maid*, which, as a set of connected short stories, was eligible for a prize exclusively for novels.

Munro was influenced in her formative years by female writers from the American South who were older contemporaries, writers such as Eudora Welty, Carson McCullers and Flannery O'Connor. These writers helped her to find her own voice both as a 'writer on the side of women' (if not a committed feminist) and as someone who wrote about rural communities. Many of Munro's stories feature the same characters, businesses and families living in the same town, giving her stories an added dimension. In this respect, she can be traced back to American regional writers, such as Kate Chopin and Sherwood Anderson.

Not surprisingly Munro's work has developed a great deal over the 30 or so years that she has been writing. Her earlier work falls more neatly into the pattern of short stories established by the modernists (see page 30), although without experiment, concentrating on a significant moment for the main character. There is plot development – these are not stories in which 'nothing ever happens' – but endings are never simple. So, 'Red Dress – 1946' (1968) concentrates on a girl's first dance and how it changes her relationship with her mother. 'Day of the Butterfly' (1968) details the disturbance of a potential relationship with the girl who is the outsider of the class. Several of the stories in Munro's first collection explore moments in the lives of children and the boundaries that they cross or fail to cross. They are straightforward narratives with no disruptions of sequence or point of view.

Later stories are more obviously complex in their structures and expansiveness. In this respect, Munro has not conformed to either the tendency towards compression or the popularity of magic realism in recent years. It became unfashionable, after the 19th century, to divide stories into sections but this is something that Munro has continued to do, especially in her longer stories, although these are not parts of a story that always unfolds in chronological order. Sometimes relating these parts together is one of the major tasks the reader has to accomplish. It has become something of a cliché to talk of the richness of Munro's stories – 'Like full-rigged sailing ships in tight-necked bottles' (Lucy Hughes-Hallett in *The Times*, 1994). Contemporary short stories work by compression, by leaving things out and suggesting much more than they actually say. But rather than pare down her stories to the bare bones as Carver does, Munro is expansive, sometimes in an apparently leisurely way, yet still manages to leave huge gaps for the reader to fill. Munro introduces several characters linked by a situation or by the narrator's perspective, so that at the beginning of a story there may be several directions in which the plot could develop. Munro seems to achieve the double act of expanding on the brevity of the traditional short story, whilst merely suggesting a larger world that the reader reconstructs.

'Cortes Island', a story from Munro's 1998 collection, *The Love of a Good Woman*, illustrates her indirect method of developing plot. A young woman (the narrator) and her husband are living in rented rooms below the Gorries, an old couple whose son owns the property. The story begins with a description of the narrator as she was at the time. It moves to a description of the Gorries' son, revealing fragments of his relationship with his mother, and then leading, by the third page, into the development of the narrator's relationship with the mother, Mrs Gorrie. Two further plot developments follow: Mrs Gorrie's husband is wheelchair bound and the narrator is looking for a job. By the third or fourth page it is still unclear which of these elements will form the main narrative strand: Munro has constructed a situation of interconnected parts, any one of which is interesting enough to carry the story.

Several critics have said that Munro breaks from the 20th-century mould of short story writing because she does not concentrate on the single moment of revelation. This is certainly true of some stories where the time span is extended, sometimes across centuries, and she uses letters and diaries to complicate issues of point of view, especially in the later stories. But often there is a central nucleus that seems to pull together the disparate parts. In 'Cortes Island', the crippled Mr Gorrie shows the narrator an old newspaper clipping about Cortes Island that seems to be connected with the narrator's resistance to conformity. In 'The Love of a Good Woman' the focusing incident is the drowning of the local optician in a river. 'A Wilderness Station' (1994) revolves around the death of a 19th-century pioneer in the wilds of Canada, using a series of letters and diaries. Readers are perhaps motivated like readers of detective stories to find answers that are often hidden in the past, and in this sense Munro creates compelling narrative lines. But the answers are never of the 'whodunnit' nature; the stories repeatedly reveal and conceal as another point of view is added. The end is often a matter of working out the relationship between the events and the characters' inner lives. Arguably Munro has reinvented the short story form by using familiar techniques such as diaries and letters and combining them with the idea of the single moment. But the single moment is often only a still centre around which the significant ideas of the story are worked out. Munro's stories are perhaps best summed up by her own phrase: '… something not startling until you think of trying to tell it.'

Angela Carter and magic realism

Angela Carter (1940–1992) was one of Britain's foremost feminist writers of recent years. She began writing novels in the 1960s and has written several novels as well as four volumes of short stories: *Fireworks* (1974), *The Bloody Chamber and Other Stories* (1979), *Black Venus* (1985), and *Come Unto these Yellow Sands* (1985). Her work is particularly known for its reworking of myth and fairy tale from a feminist point of view. That is, her stories will often retain the basic plot and structure of the original, but there may be subtle differences in point of view or in the outcome of the story. Amongst British writers she is sometimes known as the godmother of magic realism. Magic realism is popular with South American writers such as Marquez and Borges, and also with the Indian writer, Salman Rushdie. It is fiction in which the rules of the 'real world' are blatantly disregarded (people fly or fill their houses with water so that they can sail boats), but the style of realism is preserved. That is, the readers are given no special warning that what they are reading is fantasy or fairy tale (such as a 'Once upon a time' opening). Carter's magic realism is perhaps more safely grounded than that of her contemporaries because her use of the fairy tale genre prepares readers for what is to follow.

The Bloody Chamber is a collection of rewritings of well-known fairy tales such as Little Red Riding Hood, Blue Beard and Beauty and the Beast. Carter's feminist ploy is not so much to provide a sudden and humorous twist in which, for example, Little Red Riding Hood shoots the wolf, as to make subtle changes in which women's power is asserted. For example, instead of being eaten by the wolf, the girl goes to bed with him, the implication being that she tames him rather than that he is just another rampant male. Needless to say, this interpretation has been debated by feminist critics.

The sexual liberty of women in Carter's work stems from the liberal attitudes of the 1960s. It is over the role of the erotic that feminist critical opinion on Carter is most divided. For Maggie Anwell, the erotic element helps to show that women can use their sexuality to assert themselves. For others, such as Patricia Duncker, Carter moves too close to pornography for comfort. In this pornography, Duncker sees Carter as indulging in descriptions of male sadism that essentially promote and extend a male version of the world. (See Further reading, page 118.)

▶ Read 'The Snow Child' (Part 3, pages 89–90). Can it, in your view, support a feminist reading? Look closely at the parts played by the three characters and the significance of 'biting'.

▶ How useful is Margaret Atwood's interpretation of 'The Snow Child', below? Is there an epiphany? Does it confirm the view of these stories as sadistic?

> 'The Snow Child' is a brief fable in which the Count's desire for a 'perfect' virginal girl-child as sexual object materialises as a snow-child (*pace* Hawthorne), much to the distaste of the Countess. The Count dresses the snow-child in the Countess's finery, and things are looking bad for the now-naked Countess (nakedness here is poverty, not essence) until she desires a rose. The snow-child picks the rose, but it pricks her and she bleeds; the blood kills her, since she is only an idea, an idea of virginal perfection, which cannot survive actual passion. The Count has sex with the dead body anyway (take that, *Playboy* magazine!) and is soon 'finished'. The snow-child melts, and the countess has all her clothes again. But it is the rose that has become carnivorous: when the Countess touches it, 'it bites'.
>
> (Margaret Atwood in *The Flesh and the Mirror*, ed. Lorna Sage, 1994)

Short shorts: a small good thing?

> As if the titanic ego of fiction itself has been brought down to a human scale …
>
> (Charles Baxter in Shapard and Thomas, 1991)

Short short stories have received increasing attention in the last ten years as a form in their own right, although they have been written for a great deal longer. Hemingway wrote several fragments that are less than a page long and even a story called 'A Very Short Story' (1926). Well-known contemporary writers also contribute, such as Raymond Carver, John Updike, John Cheever, Joyce Carol Oates, and others. Short shorts have been popularised in literary competitions that tend to bring out a writer's ability to use verbal sleight of hand, but attempts to give them respectability have been made notably by compilers Shapard and Thomas (see Further reading, page 117). Just how short a short short has to be is a matter for debate; most of the complete stories in Part 3 would qualify on the grounds of length.

It may be that the form is as diverse as modern short stories have become. But

Baxter believes that these mini stories are a profound exploration of human nature. This is not because they expose a moral dilemma, a crucial moment of insight or a life changing choice – there is no time for that. In short short stories behaviour is a reaction, it occurs without thought and thus exposes us in 'little unexpected explosive moments'. (in Shapard and Thomas, 1991)

But why are short shorts in vogue? The idea of the three-minute culture – that the West is increasingly a culture of short attention spans – was made popular in the 1960s. But the problem here is that short shorts are as intense as poetry and often demand just as much rereading. Or is it a matter of resources? In a culture where resources are in such plenitude, is it not likely that it becomes a challenge to make do with the least? Where information is cheap, the richness of a little runs deep.

Other contemporary short story writers

These include: John Updike's dozen volumes of short stories, including *The Afterlife and Other Stories* (1995); Ian McEwan's *First Love, Last Rites* (1976); Janet Frame's first collection *The Lagoon and Other Stories* (1951) which helped secure her release from a mental institution; Muriel Spark's *Bang-Bang You're Dead and Other Stories* (1982); and William Trevor's most recent collection *The Hill Bachelors* (2000).

Assignments

1   Read 'Crazy Robin' and 'Miss Brill' (Part 3, pages 73–76 and page 83–87. Compare the two stories as examples of tales or short stories, using the criteria for tales given on page 11. To what extent do you find the distinction useful in your reading of the two stories?

2   Read George Orwell's 'Shooting an Elephant' (1950). Compare this with 'Miss Brill' or 'Crazy Robin' in terms of story telling techniques. Pay particular attention to the way the stories end. Would you consider 'Shooting an Elephant' to be a tale, a sketch, an essay or a short story?

3   The ghost story genre has often examined serious themes. Explore the ghost stories of different eras and compare them. Your starting points might be: Charles Dickens 'The Signalman'; Rudyard Kipling 'The House Surgeon'; Henry James 'The Turn of the Screw' or 'The Friends of the Friends'; A.S. Byatt 'The July Ghost'.

4   Compare images of entrapment as used by Edgar Allan Poe, Charlotte Perkins Gilman and Edith Wharton, and the uses to which they put these images in their stories.

5   To what extent do you agree with the following assessment of Hemingway's characters and their qualities? Give your views with reference to about six of his stories:

Nobody in Hemingway ever seems to have a job or a home … [His characters are] associated with recreation rather than with labour – waiters, barmen, boxers, bullfighters, and the like … Even war is treated as recreation, an amusement for the leisured classes. In these stories practically no single virtue is discussed with the exception of physical courage …'
(Frank O'Connor *The Lonely Voice*, 1963)

6   Organise the beginnings of the stories in Part 3 (pages 71–73) chronologically, and explain how you think stories have changed in style over the last 200 years. Using an anthology of short stories, examine the range of story types by reading a selection of stories from the last 200 years.

7   Sample some of Gordimer's stories from the chronologically arranged *Selected Stories* (Penguin, 1983). How would you describe the progress of her stories in terms of both theme and style? Focus on the presentation of relationships between the races and the use of epiphany (see page 103) to express this relationship.

8   Read Carver's 'The Bath' and the later expanded version 'A Small Good Thing', both in the collection *Stories* (Picador, 1985). How do you think the changes reflect Carver's development as a writer of short stories? Consider, in particular, the part played by the final scene. Does the story involve an epiphany? If so, is it for the reader or for any of the characters?

9   Based on your own reading of the stories in Angela Carter's *The Bloody Chamber*, do you feel that the presentation of sex shows women asserting themselves or another version of male superiority?

10 Compare Carter's use of fairy tale with that of Michèle Roberts in 'Anger' from the collection *During Mother's Absence* (1993) or with A.S. Byatt's *The Djinn in the Nightingale's Eye* (1994).

11 Many critics see magic realism as a kind of post-modernism. Using the criteria for post-modernism on page 42, to what extent would you regard *The Bloody Chamber* as post-modernist?

12 The stories in *The Bloody Chamber* are closely linked to traditional versions of fairy stories. How far do you feel that knowledge of traditional stories is necessary for a full understanding of Carter's work? In other words, are these stories purely intertextual or can they stand alone?

13 Make a copy of 'Snow' (Part 3, pages 92–93) and underline the metafictional elements. What does 'Snow' seem to be saying about stories?

14 William Peden defines short short stories like this:

Skinny fiction, or mini-fiction: a single episode narrative with a single setting, a brief time span, and a limited number of speaking characters (three or four at the most); a revelation-epiphany: the click of a camera, the opening or closing of a window, a moment of insight.

(in *Shapard and Thomas*, 1986)

But to what extent does this definition also apply to short stories? Consider this question with reference to about six short stories you have read.

2 | Approaching the texts

- What are the different features and techniques used by writers of modern short stories?

- How might these features and techniques influence reading and interpretation?

- How has use of these techniques changed over time?

- How does use of these techniques compare with their use in novels?

Point of view

Point of view in fiction is about who is seeing the events of the story. There are several possibilities for the storywriter, the basics of which will be covered here. The story can be told from the point of view of:

- an omniscient narrator who can move at will in and out of the heads of any of the characters

- one or two of the characters in the story

- an observer who may or may not be a part of the story.

As a general rule, if the reader follows the fortunes of a particular character, then there is a tendency to empathise with that character, whether or not the writer has allowed you into that character's thoughts. In fact, if readers have been excluded from the character's thoughts and feelings, it is likely that they will be providing these things for themselves, by making guesses from the context. This is actually typical of short story style, particularly in the 20th century, where what is left out is as important as what is put in (see **ellipsis**, page 60).

How is point of view important for reading a story? It affects what readers know about the characters, how they feel about them and consequently how they read the whole story. It is sometimes said that what contributes to the ambiguity of some of Katherine Mansfield's short stories is the fact that readers are given access to the thoughts of several of the characters, so it is difficult to know whose side the writer is on.

Short stories have often been described as 'subjective' in their approach. That is, they tend to view events from a highly restricted point of view – from one person's view of reality. Many of Poe's stories ('The Tell Tale Heart', 'The Pit and the Pendulum') are highly restricted in their point of view because this tends to reinforce the physical isolation of the character, both central to Poe's idea of the short story creating a single effect (see page 101). Readers often have to step outside the restricted point of view imposed by the writer. For example, towards the end of 'The Tell Tale Heart', the reader needs to see what is actually happening as the police question the killer, rather than just relying on the killer's distorted vision (see pages 76–80).

This 'subjective' approach has tended to support the idea of short stories being about a crucial moment in someone's life; in order to see how someone has changed it is important to understand their way of seeing things. This does not mean that most stories are written in the first person. This passage from 'Red and Green Beads' by Susan Hill is written from the point of view of the Curé:

> The Curé bent down and reburied them and for a moment did not know how he would get up again, his legs were so stiff and painful. But he managed it and walked home. It was raining. He was glad to reach his chair. Marie had only just lit the fire, the room was cold. He sat there alone for some time, thinking about Madame Curveillers and Marcel, and Marcel's gift of the red and green beads which had given him the answer to his questions.
> (from 'Red and Green Beads' in *A Bit of Singing and Dancing*, 1973)

Note that the text follows the character's actions (lines 1–2). In lines 3–4 details are introduced as that character would see them. The reader is given access to the character's thoughts in line 5.

Showing versus telling

Showing and telling are two key ideas for the way that language is used to create stories. If an author 'shows' the reader something, he or she lets the reader see it happening in the story, as, for example, when a character's actions are described or dialogue is used. In Anita Desai's story 'Games at Twilight' (1978) the author shows us children talking about playing:

> 'Let's play hide-and-seek.'
> 'Who'll be it?'
> 'You be it.'
> 'Why should I? You be – '
> 'You're the eldest – '
> 'That doesn't mean – '

The text tries to imitate life: there are no speech tags ('He said') and some utterances are left incomplete. It is not difficult to imagine the authorial 'telling' that might have accompanied this dialogue had it been written 100 years ago or more. However, a detailed description of actions could also count as showing, especially if there is no accompanying explanation.

Telling, on the other hand, involves the author telling or explaining something that might otherwise be shown in actions or dialogue:

> Such was the village. It is likely that the people of the village were insensitive: but it is more than likely that they never noticed their surroundings because they lived in a kind of perpetual enchantment.
>
> (R.K. Narayan 'Under the Banyan Tree', 1985)

Here Narayan has chosen to explain the people's behaviour, although he does offer two alternatives – insensitivity or 'perpetual enchantment', showing that the narrator is less than certain about what he says.

What is important about the distinction between showing and telling is that the author's choice affects in subtle ways how a reader might respond. When a writer 'shows', it means that the reader has to make deductions about characters, relationships and so forth. Telling means that the reader has had some of the work done by the author and so stories that tell a lot ought to be a great deal simpler. But the situation is not quite so clear cut. Too much telling would tend to block out the reader's response altogether and create a kind of story summary in which there was no tension, no questions to be answered and no real reason for reading. Much also depends on how the writer chooses to tell. Like Narayan above, the narrator may not himself be certain about his characters, or he may only tell us half of the truth. Many authors explain using such metaphorical language that this too has to be interpreted and connected with other metaphors in the story. In extreme cases, the narrator can mislead the reader, becoming an 'unreliable narrator'.

Towards the end of the 19th century, plots began to disappear, and so too did a concern with the outward action of the story. What actually happened became far less important than what was happening inside the characters' heads, their thoughts and emotions. Modernist writers began to experiment with different ways of expressing these internal worlds. Virginia Woolf tried to write down the words that might have been going through the character's head in a 'stream of consciousness', whereas Hemingway, using completely the opposite technique, avoided all mention of internal states such as thoughts and feelings, leaving the reader to infer them. So, both of these modernist writers were 'showing', but they were showing vastly different things to their readers.

Telling can take a number of forms: narrators can tell us about characters and their beliefs, attitudes, etc.; they can draw conclusions for readers; they can make philosophical or moral statements; they can make comments on the story telling itself. Which of these is the following example?

I started by saying that I wondered if I could do it and now I must tell you what it is that I have tried to do. I wanted to see whether I could hold your attention for a few pages while I drew for you the portrait of a man ...

(Somerset Maugham 'Salvatore', 1951)

The above example gives readers the impression that there is a narrator sitting behind the events of the story, controlling what happens. As the 20th century progressed, the narrator became less and less obtrusive, less directive, and scenes in stories have been left to speak for themselves – although, in post-modern fiction, there has been something of a revival of narrators.

▶ Compare 'Preservation' and 'Snow' (Part 3, pages 91–92 and pages 92–93) with respect to showing and telling. How do these differences influence you as you read?

Plotting

It is a familiar experience to watch a film and be impressed by the special effects and the acting, but to be disappointed by the plot. In this straightforward sense 'plot' is the series of events put together to make the complete story. Like disappointing films, short stories written in the last 100 years or so often disappoint readers expecting a rip-roaring plot. Plot in short stories has become less important than revealing psychology and the essence of a situation.

One simple question to ask about a story is: is this a 'plotted' story or a 'plotless' story? The distinction put this way is a little too black and white, and many stories will fall somewhere in between. Nevertheless, the distinction is a useful starting point for making decisions about plots. In a little more detail, this is what the question asks:

Plotted stories: is there a series of events for which the order is important and which ends in a conclusion that seems final and often involves a twist? The Little Red Riding Hood fairy tale would fall into this category, as would Dickens' 'The Signalman', Hardy's 'The Withered Arm', Kate Chopin's 'The Story of an Hour' and Stevenson's 'The Body Snatcher'.

Plotless stories: does the story revolve around one major event or series of minor scenes and seem to end inconclusively? Raymond Carver's 'Popular Mechanics', Hemingway's 'The End of Something', Anita Desai's 'Sale' and John Updike's 'The Carol Sing' are examples of this kind of 'plotless' story, to varying degrees.

The distinction is also useful because it helps to place many stories within their historical context. Many 19th-century short stories were plotted because they were written to be read aloud and therefore had to maintain the listeners' attention.

Short stories of the 20th century, on the other hand, assume that someone is reading and rereading them and can therefore piece together details of intricate symbolism, and so this pattern-making takes over from plot. As a general rule, if the plot is not strong then readers should look for epiphany (see page 103), asking themselves, what has this character learned during the story?

▶ Summarise the plots of 'Crazy Robin', 'Miss Brill' and 'Snow' (Part 3, pages 73–76, 83–87 and 92–93) in about six lines or so. What does this tell you about the plots of these stories and the periods in which they were written?

Ellipsis

If there is no real plot to a story, then it is a good idea to ask what is missing that would make the plot complete. Ellipsis refers to things in a story that are missed out. The fact that things are missed out is one of the most important differences between the short story and the novel, and between earlier and later short stories. One exception to this is Chekhov who actually advised writers to write a story and then delete the beginning and the end. Some examples of ellipses follow.

Stories by Hemingway often plunge the reader straight into the story without exposition (see below) or explanation, for example 'Cat in the Rain' (1928) and 'Hills Like White Elephants' (1926). Other stories may miss out part of the middle of the story or even the ending. It has become popular in the last 50 years amongst writers of realist fiction to suggest an ending without stating it explicitly. Much of what goes on when analysing such stories is that readers re-create 'the whole story' from the fragments that the writer has given them. In order to do this readers need to have some knowledge of how stories work; for example, it could be argued that in order to appreciate fully Angela Carter's rewritings of fairy tales readers must know the originals. This idea of using one story to read another is known as intertextuality. Throughout the 20th century writers expected readers to know about a range of other texts in order to read their stories.

▶ Read 'The Snow Child', 'Once Upon a Time' and 'Snow' (Part 3, pages 89–90, 94–98 and 92–93). What knowledge of stories does each writer expect her readers to have? How do the writers put this knowledge to different uses?

Beginnings

There are two extreme forms of short story beginnings: first, where readers are plunged straight into the world of the story as if they knew about it all along. Such openings make no allowance for the fact that readers actually know neither the characters nor the situation at the start of the story. Second, where the narrator takes completely the opposite view and assumes that readers need to have everything introduced. In this case, there might be an introduction to the scene and the characters before the action of the story begins – otherwise known as **exposition**.

These two styles – which are extremes and so inevitably many stories lie somewhere in between – tell us something about the history of modern short stories from the 19th century into the 20th. Exposition was favoured in the 19th century (by Hardy, for example) and in more traditionally written stories:

> The Reverend Curtis Hartman was pastor of the Presbyterian Church of Winesburg, and had been in that position ten years. He was forty years old, and by his nature very silent and reticent. To preach, standing in the pulpit before the people, was always a hardship for him and from Wednesday morning until Saturday evening he thought of nothing but the two sermons that must be preached on Sunday.
> (Sherwood Anderson 'The Strength of God' in *Winesburg Ohio*, 1919)

Exposition is typically descriptive so the verb 'to be' is much used. Before the story proper begins there will probably be a sense of routine that gives the impression of a character's life across a broad expanse of time before the particular events of the story the reader is about to experience. This background information may be very important if the main character is to be changed by the events of the story.

The contrasting style, which begins *in medias res* (in the middle of the action), grew in popularity from the time of the modernists, although it had been used before then, in the work of Kate Chopin, for example. When an *in medias res* beginning is used what happens to the background information that might have formed the exposition? There are a number of possible answers to this. The exposition may come later in a self-contained paragraph, it may be missed out completely and readers have to piece it together for themselves, or it may be distributed throughout the story.

The most extreme form of *in medias res* beginning is typical of many late 20th-century short stories and uses **cataphoric reference**. This entails the use of pronouns ('he', 'she', 'it') before their referents (the names of the people they refer to); for example, 'He longed for death, and he longed for his gramophone records to arrive. The rest of life's business was complete.' (Julian Barnes *Cross Channel*, 1998). In this example, the main character's name is not introduced for another two pages. The technique reached its peak in the stories of Hemingway and Faulkner, and this influence continued into the 1980s in the work of Raymond Carver.

In ordinary language pronouns *follow* their referents, so why does the short story reverse the order in this way? The most obvious answer to this question is to arouse readers' curiosity about the characters' identities. But there are more subtle reasons for this reversal. Much 20th-century fiction is characterised by a pessimistic view of human nature, especially in connection with relationships. It is not uncommon for people to be presented as alienated from each other and the excessive use of pronouns can contribute to a sense of anonymity; these people are not the heroes of legend – but just ordinary people who require no introduction. Pronouns also give readers a sense that they are eavesdropping on anyone's lives and this therefore contributes to the impression that the story is just a 'slice of life'.

Framing devices

In the early days of modern short stories, writers were conscious that one model for the short story was the oral tale, delivered by a story teller in front of a live audience. Indeed, many early short stories were in fact folk tales – in the sense that they were composed and passed down from one generation to the next in an oral form. Many short story writers in the 19th century sought to captivate the attention of readers and listeners in the same way that oral stories had done. As a result, these stories bear remains of the oral form. In the 1950s some Caribbean writers incorporated oral traditions into their stories as a means of expressing their nationalistic feelings.

One of the most common forms to derive from the oral tradition is the 'frame' in which a narrator (who may or may not be a character) introduces a situation in which someone else then tells the story. Hardy's 'A Tradition of Eighteen Hundred and Four' (1882) provides an example of this. It begins:

> The widely discussed possibility of an invasion of England through a Channel tunnel has more than once recalled old Solomon Selby's story to my mind.
> The occasion on which I numbered myself among his audience was one evening when he was sitting in the yawning chimney-corner of the inn-kitchen ..... Breaking off our few desultory remarks we drew up closer, and he thus began: –

This method is called a '**framing device**' because there is usually a return to the frame at the end. It was used by Kipling, Maupassant and others in the 19th century, by Somerset Maugham in the 20th century, but has declined since. There are several reasons why this device was used. It increased the believability of the story being told, or, if the story was fantastic in some way the frame acted as a 'buffer' back to the real world (as in Maupassant's 'The Hand', 1875). In an obvious sense, a frame also provided a way of beginning and ending a story, especially at a time when stories were expected to be rounded off. However, note that these reasons for using this device are not ready made answers: there is no substitute for taking into consideration each individual story you are studying.

The narrator's frame is not the only way of 'marking off' the story at the beginning and the end. A story can be framed by a recurrence of a similar scene to one at the beginning, or by the appearance of similar images. It is important to remember that repetition is never mere repetition, and is never accidental. The repetition might be the same idea in a different context, indicating that something has changed; conversely, it could indicate that nothing has changed as a result of the events of the story.

V.S. Naipaul's story 'The Nightwatchman's Occurrence Book' (1969) consists entirely of the written reports from a nightwatchman with replies from his manager. It recounts the conflicts between these two as events in the hotel at night become more and more chaotic and the reports correspondingly complicated. The story is framed by two simple, factual reports, thus showing that the story has gone full circle. This could be taken to imply different things: that in a position of powerlessness it is best for the nightwatchman just to keep quiet; it could imply the inevitability of class divisions; the simple reportage, in contrast to the opinions expressed in the rest of the story, could imply 'know your position', in terms of social class.

▶ How does Gordimer's story 'Once Upon a Time' (Part 3, pages 94–98) make use of a framing device? Consider how she has adapted the framing device for her own purposes.

▶ Some theorists see post-modern stories as like 'broken frames'. Read 'Once Upon a Time' and 'Snow' (Part 3, pages 94–98 and pages 92–93) and respond to the appropriateness of this description.

It is sometimes useful to compare the beginnings of novels with the beginnings of short stories. If short stories have a unique style then it should, by and large, be possible to distinguish a short story from a novel on the basis of its beginning. Here are some distinguishing features:

- Short stories are more likely to start *in medias res*.
- Short stories are much more likely to use cataphoric reference.
- Short stories are much more likely to use a framing device.
- The time span described in a short story is likely to be shorter than that of a novel.
- The spatial frame of reference is likely to be narrower in a short story.

- It is more difficult to distinguish between 20th-century novels and short stories.

▶ Read the beginnings of stories in Part 3, pages 71–73. Discuss which you think is a short story and which is a novel, giving reasons for your decisions.

Endings

The ending of a short story is probably more important than its beginning. Short stories have been called a form of writing in which the end is always present, lurking behind the action and exerting its influence in the reader's expectations. When you read a novel, you are not constantly aware of how it might end: there is too much else to be experienced before the end is reached. With a short story, however, the end will come sooner and, arguably, is a weightier part of the overall design because it influences the way that the reader interprets the rest of the story.

What follows is a list of various types of endings. It is not exhaustive and it does not account for subtle variations, of which there are many. The list is a starting point.

Return to frame/explicit explanation

It was pointed out on page 62 that there is often a return to the frame, once that technique has been used at the beginning. In Maupassant's 'Mother Savage' the story is being told by Serval to the frame narrator. The story ends with comments on the story from Serval and the frame narrator:

> My friend Serval added: 'It was by way of reprisal that the German's destroyed the local chateau, which belonged to me.'
> I for my part was thinking of the mothers of the four gentle boys burned in there, and of the fearful heroism of that other mother, shot against that wall.
> And I picked up a little stone, still blackened by the fire.

These comments give the story a sense of completion, and the reference to the stone is a confirmation of how 'close' to the two men the events of the story are. However, narrator comments at the end of a story should not be taken as definitive interpretations of a story. On the contrary, they should themselves be interpreted, acting as starting points rather than conclusions. Thus, the narrator at the end of Dickens' 'The Signalman' points out the coincidences that the alert reader should have noticed, but discussion of the interpretation of this story will go far beyond the narrator's brief signposting. Indeed, one may ask what motivates the particular comments by the narrator. Do they avoid the central issue? Do they show a bias in the thinking displayed? Does the author intend the explanation to be flawed?

A variation on 'return to the frame' is 'return to the present'. There need not be any explanation or comment from the narrator. The story simply catches up with the present, assuming that the main story was in the past. Notice that the last sentence in the example below is written in the present tense:

> Their graves were dug at the back of the little church, near the wall. There is no memorial to mark the spot, but Phyllis pointed it out to me. While she lived she used to keep their mounds neat; but now they are overgrown with nettles, and sunk nearly flat. The older villagers, however, who know of the episode from their parents, still recollect the place where the soldiers lie. Phyllis lies near.
>
> (Thomas Hardy 'The Melancholy Hussar of the German Legion,' 1889)

The reader should be aware of the emotions evoked by such an ending and make a comparison with the narrator's attitude at the beginning of the story.

Symbols

Frequently stories end with a few lines that seem to have little to do with the plot. They may focus on some detail of the situation, an action, an object perhaps, or on an aspect of one of the characters. This means that a story ends with an apparently irrelevant statement that usually has some symbolic significance. The method has become popular in short stories as suggestion and ambiguity rather than explicit statement of meaning have become prominent.

> He went on down the hill, toward the dark wood within which the liquid silver voices of the birds called unceasing – the rapid and urgent beating of the urgent and quiring heart of the late spring night. He did not look back.
>
> (William Faulkner 'Barn Burning', 1939)

Sometimes symbolic significance is fairly obvious. In the above example, 'not looking back' probably symbolises a rejection of the past. On other occasions the symbolism will have to be worked out from the context.

▶ Compare the use of symbols at the end of 'The Snow Child' and 'Snow' (Part 3, pages 89–90 and 92–93): 'biting' and 'the heart' respectively. Discuss the significance of these symbols for the rest of the story in which they appear. Which one do you find easiest to integrate?

Irony

This is treated separately from either 'summary' or 'twist' because the **irony** can work in a number of different ways. Irony occurs essentially when a story seems to say the opposite of what it means. It is not a way to produce a happy ending because the irony often exposes some course of action as ridiculous, misguided or tragic. This reflects a 20th-century way of thinking. Carver's 'Popular Mechanics' (1982) is a very brief story about a man and woman who argue, and who kill their baby as a result. This bleak conclusion is only stated indirectly in the closing line: 'And in this manner, the issue was decided.'

The irony derives from the neutral, detached tone in which this is stated, and in the painful truth of the word 'decided', which is no decision at all on this occasion. The irony is further reinforced by the story's intertextual reference to the King Solomon story from the Old Testament of the Bible. Solomon ('the wise') is asked by two women to decide which of them is the true mother of the baby before them. In order to discover the truth, Solomon offers to cut the baby in half so that they can share it, whereupon the true mother protests, saying that the other woman can have her baby rather than kill it. In the Biblical version, the idea of splitting of the baby solves the problem, but in Carver's 20th-century version it is the disastrous conclusion. The irony reflects Carver's bleak vision of modern urban life.

▶ Which of the longer extracts and stories in Part 3 do you regard as having ironic endings?

Summary of events

Such a summary might provide a missing piece of the action and also act as an explanation for what has happened earlier in the story. In Evelyn Waugh's (1903–1966) story 'Mr Loveday's Little Outing' (1936), a long-term psychiatric patient has been secured release by the main character of the story. But to everyone's surprise he returns to the home within two hours:

> Half a mile up the road from the asylum gates, they later discovered an abandoned bicycle. It was a lady's machine of some antiquity. Quite near it in the ditch lay the strangled body of a young woman, who, riding home to her tea, had chanced to overtake Mr Loveday, as he strode along, musing on his opportunities.

This summary resolves the story neatly for the reader without explicitly stating that the inmate was still a psychopathic killer, in spite of appearances to the contrary. The restraint of 'chanced to overtake' and 'musing on his opportunities' can be seen as both humorous and dark in intent. The tone also echoes the harmlessness of the title, 'Mr Loveday's Little Outing'. The effect is one of irony which casts a shadow over much of the details of the whole story. This is a good example of a 'twist' that creates irony – with which the short story has come to be associated.

Change of point of view

This method works in a similar way to the symbolic ending in that can cast the events of the story in a new light. V.S. Pritchett's 'A Family Man' (from *On the Edge of the Cliff*, 1979) is the story of a woman who lies to escape the accusations of her lover's wife. The whole story is narrated from the woman's point of view until the very last paragraph when she goes to visit the Brewsters, who comment:

> 'She's getting odd. She ought to get married,' Mrs Brewster said. 'I wish she wouldn't swoosh her hair around like that. She'd look better if she put it up.'

This statement would seem to call into question the woman's beauty, which has been connected with her truthfulness throughout the story, and the status of 'truth' is an important theme here. This again illustrates the power of endings to affect the whole reading.

The twist

The 'twist in the tale' has become one of the most popularised features of modern short stories. For that reason it has often been associated with the sensation story, most recently connected with Roald Dahl (1916–1990), or with the popular fiction of magazines, frequently appearing as romantic stories in women's magazines. These associations have led to 'the twist' being the poor relation of short story endings, and the tag has extended to the stories themselves. But the disparaging label is not always deserved and it has its roots in 19th-century classics.

Poe has been named as the originator of such stories, but this is only partly true. Poe's stories sometimes end with a surprise but equally often, if not more often, with inevitable horror. Neither were Poe's stories particularly strong on plot; they were typically detailed, almost obsessive accounts by men in bizarre predicaments, providing only scant details as to how they arrived there. These plots tended to be in two-part structures: man in predicament – man gets out of it (or not). And Poe was not particularly concerned with the manner in which the second part happened, whereas the cleverly designed twist grows inevitably (but unpredictably) from earlier details. Besides, the technique of dramatic reversal of fortune is an essential ingredient of tragedy and is therefore as old as the writings of Aristotle (384–322 BC). As far as the short story is concerned, the twist was developed far more by the Scottish writer Saki, by Maupassant in particular, and by Kate Chopin and O. Henry (1862–1910).

Dismissal of the twist as 'cheap' only really emerged in the 20th century when the division between popular stories and 'art' stories grew wider. At the beginning of the 20th century, with the advent of modernism, stories without plots came to be written by writers of calibre, and so more value was attached to this form. As the 20th century progressed, readers and critics also began to value stories that were intricate enough to stand up to close scrutiny, plot therefore taking second place.

Repetition

V.S. Pritchett said that one of the great principles of story telling is to appear to do the same thing twice, but on the second occasion to make a significant alteration. There is no doubt that the search for repetition of various kinds can provide the key to interpretation. Here are some of the things a writer might repeat:

- a significant word or phrase
- an important idea
- a scene or action.

Repetition of a scene can create a story frame, as in Naipaul's 'The Nightwatchman's Occurrence Book' (see page 48). In a completely different way, Hemingway makes frequent use of repetition. This is partly because of the simplicity of his language and his imitation of spoken style. But much of his repetition creates effects specific to their moment of occurrence in a story. Many repetitions are of mundane words like 'cold', 'dark', 'often', but Hemingway will often build them up over a paragraph and bring them all together at the end. The effect is subtle and cumulative, rather like the effect of a repeated phrase in music. Most of his stories work in this way, but a few are particularly fruitful for analysis: 'Now I Lay Me' (1928), 'In Another Country' (1928) and 'Hills Like White Elephants' (1928).

Assignments

1   Deborah Thomas (*Dickens and the Short Story*, 1982) sees Dickens as building on the oral tradition in his short stories. Compare the ways in which Dickens and Thomas Hardy make use of the oral tradition in their short stories, using a selection from both authors.

2   Read the extract from Elizabeth Bowen's 'Maria' (Part 3, pages 88–89). What points of view are used in this story? How does this influence the reader's sympathies?

3 What kind of ending does the extract from 'Tickets Please!' use (Part 3, pages 81–83)? Compare it with the endings on pages 64–67. Rewrite Lawrence's ending by experimenting with alternatives whilst keeping the effect roughly the same. Use your rewritten version to evaluate Lawrence's original ending.

4 Read Mansfield's 'Miss Brill' (Part 3, pages 83–87). Whose point of view is represented? What effect does this have on the reader at various points in the story? Why do you think that Mansfield did not write this story in the first person? Compare this story with the point of view in 'The Tell-Tale Heart' (Part 3, pages 76–80).

5 Virginia Woolf's story 'Kew Gardens' (1918) is a classic example of a pattern of images replacing plot. Read the story (in *The Penguin Book of English Short Stories*, ed. Dolley, 1967) and make notes on the pattern of the story using these guidelines:
   • the story can be divided into eight sections
   • some sections refer to humans, some to aspects of nature
   • there are several different kinds of couples represented in the story
   • the overall pattern is symmetrical.
How does the pattern contribute to your reading of the story?

6 One way of discovering what a story misses out is to summarise the action in a few lines. Two questions are then worth asking: what does the original text leave out compared with the summary? What does the summary itself lack as an alternative to the story? Try summarising any of the complete stories in Part 3. How does the story 'Snow' on pages 92–93 help you to reflect on the nature of stories?

7 Conduct a survey of the use of cataphoric reference in a range of short story collections or using the beginnings of stories on pages 71–73. Compare three collections from different periods of history, different movements (for example, modernist, post-modernist) or by male and female writers. Follow up some stories in detail to see how the use of cataphoric reference influences readings of the characters and the situation.

8 Read the beginnings of stories on pages 71–73. Identify the kinds of beginnings used by these writers as: exposition, *in medias res*, cataphoric reference, framing device, or some combination of these possibilities.

9 Read 'Crazy Robin' (pages 73–76) and 'The Tell-Tale Heart' (pages 76–80), paying particular attention to the endings of these stories. The first of these illustrates the style of many stories written before modern short stories emerged in the 19th century, while the second is one of Poe's classics of the form. Study both stories carefully, then list the major differences between them. Make notes on the following:
   • the morality conveyed by the narrator
   • the relationship between the ending and the rest of the story
   • the way in which the narrator rounds off the story
   • the way in which the narrator conveys an attitude towards the events of the story.

10 Using your conclusions from Assignment 9 above, write an analysis of some of the ways in which Poe's stories differed from what had gone before.

11 Compare the types of endings used by Kipling, Lawrence and Carver in the extracts in Part 3. Pay particular attention to the degree of resolution, point of view, the emotions evoked and the organisation of time.

12 O. Henry's story 'The Gift of the Magi' is a classic story with a twist. Obtain a copy of this and analyse how pairs of ideas contribute to the final twist. Henry adds a philosophical comment from the narrator in the final paragraph. How satisfying do you find this?

13 Repetition of words, phrases and ideas plays a key part in 'Once Upon a Time' and 'Preservation'. Find out what has been repeated and what the effect of it might be.

14 Three stories with the same title, 'The Model', illustrate differences in style and attitude between different periods. They are by Bernard Malamud (in *Sudden Fiction International*, 1991), by Maupassant (in *Selected Short Stories*, 1971), and by Joyce Carol Oates (in *Haunted – Tales of the Grotesque*, 1994). Read them and carry out an extended study using information from this book.

3 | Stories and extracts

The texts and extracts that follow have been chosen to illustrate key ideas and short story styles over 200 years. They include a mixture of familiar and unfamiliar texts and are arranged chronologically.

Beginnings

The seven extracts below are taken from the beginnings of a range of short stories and novels. The stories and writers are identified on page 99.

Extract 1

My father's family name being Pirrip, and my Christian name Philip, my infant tongue could make of both names nothing longer or more explicit than Pip. So, I called myself Pip, and came to be called Pip. I give Pirrip as my father's family name, on the authority of his tombstone and my sister – Mrs Joe Gargery, who married the blacksmith. As I never saw my father or my mother, and never saw any likeness of either of them (for their days were long before the days of photography), my first fancies regarding what they were like, were unreasonably derived from their tombstones.

Extract 2

Here stretch the downs, high and breezy and green, absolutely unchanged since those eventful days. A plough has never disturbed the turf, and the sod that was uppermost then is uppermost now. Here stood the camp; here are distinct traces of the banks thrown up for the horses of the cavalry, and spots where the midden-heaps lay are still to be observed. At night when I walk across the lonely place, it is impossible to avoid hearing, amid the scouring of the wind over the grass-bents and thistles, the old trumpet and bugle calls, the rattle of the halters; to help seeing rows of spectral tents and the impedimenta of soldiery. From within the canvases come guttural syllables of foreign tongues, and broken songs of the fatherland; for they were mainly regiments of the King's German Legion that slept round the tent-poles hereabout at that time.

Extract 3

The thousand injuries of Fortunato I had borne as I best could, but when he ventured upon insult I vowed revenge. You, who so well know the nature of my soul, will not suppose, however, that I gave utterance to a threat. At length I would be avenged; this was a point definitely settled, but the very definitiveness with which it was resolved precluded the idea of risk. I must not only punish but punish with impunity. A wrong is unredressed when retribution over-takes its redresser. It is equally unredressed when the avenger fails to make himself felt as such to him who has done the wrong.

Extract 4

He stood awkwardly, shifting his weight from one foot to the other, looking through the open pantry window with the dancing eyes of a boy about to receive a treat of good things. But it wasn't the jam tarts that the maid, Miranda, was taking hot from the oven and putting in a dish that held his gaze, rapt. It was Miranda herself, flicking her fingers smartly and putting them to her mouth as the hot baking tin burnt them.

Extract 5

'Yes,' said the dealer, 'our windfalls are of various kinds. Some customers are ignorant, and then I touch a dividend on my superior knowledge. Some are dishonest,' and here he held up the candle, so that the light fell strongly on his visitor, 'and in that case,' he continued, 'I profit by my virtue.'

Markheim had but just entered from the daylight streets, and his eyes had not yet grown familiar with the mingled shine and darkness in the shop. At these pointed words, and before the near presence of the flame, he blinked painfully and looked aside.

Extract 6

Immediately on wishing my mother dead and seeing the pain it caused her, I was sorry and cried so many tears that all the earth around me was drenched. Standing before my mother, I begged her forgiveness, and I begged so earnestly that she took pity on me, kissing my face and placing my head on her bosom, until finally I suffocated. I lay on her bosom, breathless, for a time uncountable, until one day, for a reason she has kept to herself, she shook me out and stood me under a tree and I started to breathe again. I cast a sharp glance at her and said to myself, 'So.' Instantly I grew my own bosoms, small mounds at first, leaving a small, soft place between them, where, if ever necessary, I could rest my own head. Between my mother and me now were the tears I had cried, and I gathered up some stones and banked them in so that they formed a small pond. The water in the pond was thick and black and poisonous, so that only unnamable invertebrates could live in it. My mother and I now watched each other carefully, always making sure to shower the other with words and deeds of love and affection.

Extract 7

One evening of late summer, before the nineteenth century had reached one-third of its span, a young man and a woman, the latter carrying a child, were approaching the large village of Weydon-Priors, in Upper Wessex, on foot. They were plainly but not ill clad, though the thick hoar of dust which had accumulated on their shoes and garments from an obviously long journey lent disadvantageous shabbiness to their appearance just now.

Mary Wollstonecraft

'Crazy Robin' (1788)

'Crazy Robin' is included here to illustrate the style and content of stories written before the modern short story emerged. The story is told by Mrs Mason to a group of children as they sit outside a small cave. She tells the story of Crazy Robin, a good man who is driven to madness and eventually death by a series of misfortunes.

In the afternoon the children bounded over the short grass of the common, and walked under the shadow of the mountain till they came to a craggy part; where a stream broke out, and ran down the declivity, struggling with the huge stones which impeded its progress, and occasioned a noise that did not unpleasantly interrupt the solemn silence of the place. The brook was soon lost in the neighbouring wood, and the children turned their eyes to the broken side of the mountain, over which ivy grew in great profusion. Mrs Mason pointed out a little cave, and desired them to sit down on some stumps of trees, whilst she related the promised story.

'In yonder cave once lived a poor man, who generally went by the name of Crazy Robin. In his youth he was very industrious, and married my father's dairy-maid; a girl deserving of such a good husband. For some time they continued to live very comfortably; their daily labour procured their daily bread; but Robin, finding it was likely he should have a large family, borrowed a trifle, to add to the small pittance which they had saved in service, and took a little farm in a neighbouring county. I was then a child.

'Ten or twelve years after, I heard that a crazy man, who appeared very harmless, had piled by the side of a brook a great number of stones; he would wade into the river for them, followed by a cur dog, whom he would frequently call his Jacky, and even his Nancy; and then mumble to himself – thou wilt not leave me – we will dwell with the owls in the ivy. – A number of owls had taken shelter in it. The stones which he waded for he carried to the mouth of the hole, and only just left enough room to creep in. Some of the neighbours at last recollected his face; and I sent to inquire what misfortune had reduced him to such a deplorable state.

'The information I received from different persons, I will communicate to you in as few words as I can.

'Several of his children died in their infancy; and, two years before he came to his native place, one misfortune had followed another till he had sunk under their accumulated weight. Through various accidents he was long in arrears to his landlord; who, seeing that he was an honest man, who endeavoured to bring up his family, did not distress him; but when his wife was lying-in of her last child, the landlord dying, his heir sent and seized the stock for the rent; and the person from whom he had borrowed some money, exasperated to see all gone, arresting him immediately, he was hurried to jail, without being able to leave any money for his family. The poor woman could not see them starve, and trying to support her children before she had sufficient strength, she caught cold; and through neglect, and her want of proper nourishment, her illness turned to a putrid fever; which two of the children caught from her, and died with her. The two who were left, Jacky and Nancy, went to their father, and took with them a cur dog, that had long shared their frugal meals.

'The children begged in the day, and at night slept with their wretched father. Poverty and dirt soon robbed their cheeks of the roses which the country air made bloom with a peculiar freshness; so that they soon caught a jail fever – and died. The poor father, who was now bereft of all his children, hung over their bed in speechless anguish; not a groan or a tear escaped from him, while he stood, two or three hours, in the same attitude, looking at the dead bodies of his little darlings. The dog licked his hands, and strove to attract his attention; but for a while he seemed not to observe his caresses; when he did, he said, mournfully, thou wilt not leave me – and then he began to laugh. The bodies were removed; and he remained in an unsettled state, often frantic; at length the frenzy subsided, and he grew melancholy and harmless. He was not then so closely watched; and one day he contrived to make his escape, the dog followed him, and came directly to his native village.

'After I had received this account, I determined he should live in the place he had chosen, undisturbed. I sent some conveniences, all of which he rejected, except a mat; on which he sometimes slept – and the dog always did. I tried to induce him to eat, but he constantly gave the dog whatever I sent him, and lived on haws and blackberries, and every kind of trash. I used to call frequently on him; and he sometimes followed me to the house I now live in, and in winter he would come of his own accord, and take a crust of bread. He gathered water-cresses out of the pool, and would bring them to me, with nosegays of wild thyme, which he plucked from the sides of the mountain. I mentioned before, that the dog was a cur. It had, indeed, the bad trick of a cur, and would run barking after horses' heels. One day, when his master was gathering water-cresses, the dog running after a young gentleman's horse, made it start, and almost threw the rider; who grew so angry that though he knew it was the poor madman's dog, he levelled his gun at his head – shot him – and instantly rode off. Robin ran to his dog – he looked at his wounds, and not sensible that he was dead, called to him to follow him; but when he found he could not, he took him to the pool, and washed off the blood before it began to clot, and then brought him home, and laid him on the mat.

'I observed that I had not seen him pacing up the hills as usual, and sent to inquire about him. He was found sitting by the dog, and no entreaties could prevail on him to quit the body, or receive any refreshment. I instantly set off for this place, hoping, as I had always been a favourite, that I should be able to persuade him to eat something. But when I came to him, I found that the hand of death was upon him. He was still melancholy; yet there was not such a mixture of wildness in it as formerly. I pressed him to take some food; but, instead of answering me, or turning away, he burst into tears – a thing I had never seen him do before, and, sobbing, he said, Will anyone be kind to me! – you will kill me! – I saw not my wife die – No! – they dragged me from her – but I saw Jacky and Nancy die – and who pitied me? – but my dog! He turned his eyes to the body – I wept with him. He would then have taken some nourishment, but nature was exhausted – and he expired.'

'Was that the cave?' said Mary. They ran to it. 'Poor Robin! Did you ever hear of anything so cruel?' 'Yes,' answered Mrs Mason; 'and as we walk home I will relate an instance of still greater barbarity.'

'I told you, that Robin was confined in a jail. In France they have a dreadful one, called the Bastille. The poor wretches who are confined in it live entirely alone; they have not the pleasure of seeing men or animals; nor are they allowed books. – They live in comfortless solitude. Some have amused themselves by making figures on the wall; and others have laid straws in rows. One miserable captive found a spider; he nourished it for two or three years; it grew tame, and partook of his lonely meal. The keeper observed it, and mentioned the circumstance to a superior, who ordered him to crush it. In vain did the man beg to have his spider spared. You find, Mary, that the nasty creature which you despised was a comfort in solitude. The keeper obeyed the cruel command; and the unhappy wretch felt more pain when he heard the crush, than he had ever experienced during his long confinement. He looked round a dreary apartment, and the small portion of light which the grated bars admitted, only served to show him, that he breathed where nothing else drew breath.'

Edgar Allan Poe

‘The Tell-Tale Heart’ (1845)

This story is a detailed account of a murder by a narrator who insists that he is not mad. The police arrive and the narrator tries to convince them of his innocence in the very room in which the body is hidden under the floorboards.

True! – nervous, very, very dreadfully nervous I had been and am; but why will you say that I am mad? The disease had sharpened my senses, not destroyed, not dulled them. Above all was the sense of hearing acute. I heard all things in the heaven and in the earth. I heard many things in hell. How then am I mad? Hearken! and observe how healthily, how calmly, I can tell you the whole story.

It is impossible to say how first the idea entered my brain, but, once conceived, it haunted me day and night. Object there was none. Passion there was none. I loved the old man. He had never wronged me. He had never given me insult. For his gold I had no desire. I think it was his eye! Yes, it was this! One of his eyes resembled that of a vulture – a pale blue eye with a film over it. Whenever it fell upon me my blood ran cold, and so by degrees, very gradually, I made up my mind to take the life of the old man, and thus rid myself of the eye for ever.

Now this is the point. You fancy me mad. Madmen know nothing. But you should have seen me. You should have seen how wisely I proceeded – with what caution – with what foresight, with what dissimulation, I went to work! I was never kinder to the old man than during the whole week before I killed him. And every night about midnight I turned the latch of his door and opened it oh, so gently! And then, when I had made an opening sufficient for my head, I put in a dark lantern all closed, closed so that no light shone out, and then I thrust in my head. Oh, you would have laughed to see how cunningly I thrust it in! I moved it slowly, very, very slowly, so that I might not disturb the old man's sleep. It took me an hour to place my whole head within the opening so far that I could see him as he lay upon his bed. Ha! would a madman have been so wise as this? And then when my head was well in the room I undid the lantern cautiously – oh, so cautiously – cautiously (for the hinges creaked), I undid it just so much that a single thin ray fell upon the vulture eye. And this I did for seven long nights, every night just at midnight, but I found the eye always closed, and so it was impossible to do the work, for it was not the old man who vexed me but his Evil Eye. And every morning, when the day broke, I went boldly into the chamber and spoke courageously to him, calling him by name in a hearty tone, and inquiring how he had passed the night. So you see he would have been a very profound old man, indeed, to suspect that every night, just at twelve, I looked in upon him while he slept.

Upon the eighth night I was more than usually cautious in opening the door. A watch's minute hand moves more quickly than did mine. Never before that night had I felt the extent of my own powers, of my sagacity. I could scarcely contain my feelings of triumph. To think that there I was opening the door little by little, and he not even to dream of my secret deeds or thoughts. I fairly chuckled at the idea, and perhaps he heard me, for he moved on the bed suddenly as if startled. Now you may think that I drew back – but no. His room was as black as pitch with the thick darkness (for the shutters were close fastened through fear of robbers), and so I knew that he could not see the opening of the door, and I kept pushing it on steadily, steadily.

I had my head in, and was about to open the lantern, when my thumb slipped upon the tin fastening , and the old man sprang up in the bed, crying out, 'Who's there?'

I kept quite still and said nothing. For a whole hour I did not move a muscle, and in the meantime I did not hear him lie down. He was still sitting up in the bed, listening; just as I have done night after night hearkening to the death watches in the wall.

Presently, I heard a slight groan, and I knew it was the groan of mortal terror. It was not a groan of pain or of grief – oh, no! It was the low stifled sound that arises from the bottom of the soul when overcharged with awe. I knew the sound well. Many a night, just at midnight, when all the world slept, it has welled up from my own bosom, deepening, with its dreadful echo, the terrors that distracted me. I say I knew it well. I knew what the old man felt, and pitied him although I chuckled at heart. I knew that he had been lying awake ever since the first slight noise when he had turned in the bed. His fears had been ever since growing upon him. He had been trying to fancy them causeless, but could not. He had been saying to himself, 'It is nothing but the wind in the chimney, it is only a mouse crossing the floor,' or, 'It is merely a cricket which has made a single chirp.' Yes he has been trying to comfort himself with these suppositions ; but he had found all in vain. All in vain, because Death in approaching him had stalked with his black shadow before him and enveloped the victim. And it was the mournful influence of the unperceived shadow that caused him to feel, although he neither saw nor heard, to feel the presence of my head within the room.

When I had waited a long time very patiently without hearing him lie down, I resolved to open a little – a very, very little crevice in the lantern. So I opened it – you cannot imagine how stealthily, stealthily – until at length a single dim ray like the thread of the spider shot out from the crevice and fell upon the vulture eye.

It was open, wide, wide open, and I grew furious as I gazed upon it. I saw it with perfect distinctness – all a dull blue with a hideous veil over it that chilled the very marrow in my bones, but I could see nothing else of the old man's face or person, for I had directed the ray as if by instinct precisely upon the damned spot.

And now have I not told you that what you mistake for madness is but over-acuteness of the senses? now, I say, there came to my ears a low, dull, quick sound, such as a watch makes when enveloped in cotton. I knew that sound well too. It was the beating of the old man's heart. It increased my fury as the beating of a drum stimulates the soldier into courage.

But even yet I refrained and kept still. I scarcely breathed. I held the lantern motionless. I tried how steadily I could maintain the ray upon the eye. Meantime the hellish tattoo of the heart increased. It grew quicker and quicker, and louder and louder, every instant. The old man's terror must have been extreme! It grew louder, I say, louder every moment! – do you mark me well? I have told you that I am nervous: so I am. And now at the dead hour of the night, amid the dreadful silence of that old house, so strange a noise as this excited me to uncontrollable terror. Yet, for some minutes longer I refrained and stood still. But the beating grew louder, louder! I thought the heart must burst. And now a new anxiety seized me – the sound would be heard by a neighbour! The old man's hour had come! With a loud yell, I threw open the lantern and leaped into the room. He shrieked once – once only. In an instant I dragged him to the floor, and pulled the heavy bed over him. I then smiled gaily, to find the deed so far done. But for many minutes the heart beat on with a muffled sound. This, however, did not vex me; it would not be heard through the wall. At length it ceased. The old man was dead. I removed the bed and examined the corpse. Yes, he was stone, stone dead. I placed my hand upon the heart and held it there many minutes. There was no pulsation. He was stone dead. His eye would trouble me no more.

If still you think me mad, you will think so no longer when I describe the wise precautions I took for the concealment of the body. The night waned, and I worked hastily, but in silence.

I took up three planks from the flooring of the chamber, and deposited all between the scantlings. I then replaced the boards so cleverly so cunningly, that no human eye – not even his – could have detected anything wrong. There was nothing to wash out – no stain of any kind – no blood-spot whatever. I had been too wary for that.

When I had made an end of these labours, it was four o'clock – still dark as midnight. As the bell sounded the hour, there came a knocking at the street door. I went down to open it with a light heart, – for what had I now to fear? There entered three men, who introduced themselves, with perfect suavity, as officers of the police. A shriek had been heard by a neighbour during the night; suspicion of foul play had been aroused; information had been lodged at the police office, and they (the officers) had been deputed to search the premises.

I smiled, – for what had I to fear? I bade the gentlemen welcome. The shriek, I said, was my own in a dream. The old man, I mentioned, was absent in the country. I took my visitors all over the house. I bade them search – search well. I led them, at length, to his chamber. I showed them his treasures, secure, undisturbed. In the enthusiasm of my confidence, I brought chairs into the room, and desired them here to rest from their fatigues, while I myself, in the wild audacity of my perfect triumph, placed my own seat upon the very spot beneath which reposed the corpse of the victim.

The officers were satisfied. My manner had convinced them. I was singularly at ease. They sat and while I answered cheerily, they chatted of familiar things. But, ere long, I felt myself getting pale and wished them gone. My head ached, and I fancied a ringing in my ears; but still they sat, and still chatted. The ringing became more distinct: I talked more freely to get rid of the feeling: but it continued and gained definitiveness – until, at length, I found that the noise was not within my ears.

No doubt I now grew very pale; – but I talked more fluently, and with a heightened voice. Yet the sound increased – and what could I do? It was a *low, dull, quick sound – much such a sound as a watch makes when enveloped in cotton*. I gasped for breath – and yet the officers heard it not. I talked more quickly – more vehemently; but the noise steadily increased. I arose and argued about trifles, in a high key and with violent gesticulations, but the noise steadily increased. Why would they not be gone? I paced the floor to and fro with heavy strides, as if excited to fury by the observation of the men – but the noise steadily increased. Oh God! What *could* I do? I foamed – I raved – I swore! I swung the chair on which I had been sitting, and grated it upon the boards, but the noise arose over all and continually increased. It grew louder – louder – *louder*! And still the men chatted pleasantly, and smiled. Was it possible they heard it not? Almighty God! – no, no! They heard! – they suspected! – they knew! – they were making a mockery of my horror! – this I thought, and this I think. But any thing was better than this agony! Any thing was more tolerable than this derision! I could bear those hypocritical smiles no longer! I felt that I must scream or die! – and now – again! hark! louder! louder! louder! louder! –

"Villains!" I shrieked, "dissemble no more! I admit the deed! – tear up the planks! – here, here! – it is the beating of his hideous heart!"

Rudyard Kipling

From 'Lispeth' (1888)

An Indian girl from the Himalayas has been taken in by the local Christian missionaries. Lispeth (a corruption of Elizabeth) suddenly falls in love with an Englishman and intends to marry him. This early story of Kipling's builds on his experiences as a reporter during the British Raj and on his knowledge of both races.

At the end of three months Lispeth made daily pilgrimage to Narkunda to see if her Englishman was coming along the road. It gave her comfort, and the Chaplain's wife finding her happier thought that she was getting over her 'barbarous and most indelicate folly'. A little later the walks ceased to help Lispeth, and her temper grew very bad. The Chaplain's wife thought this a profitable time to let her know the real state of affairs – that the Englishman had only promised his love to keep her quiet – that he had never meant anything, and it was wrong and improper of Lispeth to think of marriage with an Englishman, who was of superior clay, besides being promised in marriage to a girl of his own people. Lispeth said that all this was clearly impossible because he had said that he loved her, and the Chaplain's wife had, with her own lips, asserted that the Englishman was coming back.

'How can what he and you said be untrue?' asked Lispeth.

'We said it as an excuse to keep you quiet, child,' said the Chaplain's wife.

'The you have lied to me,' said Lispeth, 'you and he?'

The Chaplain's wife bowed her head, and said nothing. Lispeth was silent too for a little time; then she went out down the valley, and returned in the dress of a Hill-girl – infamously dirty, but without the nose-stud and ear-rings. She had her hair braided into the long pigtail, helped out with black thread, that Hill-women wear.

'I am going back to my own people,' said she. 'You have killed Lispeth. There is only left old Jadéh's daughter – the daughter of a *pahari* and the servant of a *Tarka Devi*. You are all liars, you English.'

By the time that the Chaplain's wife had recovered from the shock of the announcement that Lispeth had 'verted to her mother's gods the girl had gone; and she never came back.

She took to her own unclean people savagely, as if to make up the arrears of the life she had stepped out of; and, in a little time, she married a woodcutter who beat her after the manner of *paharis*, and her beauty faded soon.

'There is no law whereby you can account for the vagaries of the heathen,' said the Chaplain's wife, 'and I believe that Lispeth was always at heart an infidel.' Seeing she had been taken into the Church of England at the mature age of five weeks, this statement does not do credit to the Chaplain's wife.

Lispeth was a very old woman when she died. She had always a perfect command of English, and when she was sufficiently drunk could sometimes be induced to tell the story of her first love-affair.

It was hard then to realise that the bleared, wrinkled creature, exactly like a wisp of charred rag, could ever have been 'Lispeth of the Kotgarh Mission'.

D.H. Lawrence

From 'Tickets Please!' (1922)

John Thomas, an inspector at the bus station, has been dating the female conductors that work for him and treating them unfairly. Annie and the others decide to take revenge on Thomas by locking him in a room and forcing him to choose one of them to take out.

'You ought to be *killed*, that's what you ought,' said Annie, tensely. 'You ought to be *killed*.' And there was a terrifying lust in her voice.

Polly was ceasing to laugh, and giving long drawn Oh-h-hs and sighs as she came to herself.

'He's got to choose,' she said vaguely.

'Oh, yes, he has,' said Laura, with vindictive decision.

'Do you hear – do you hear?' said Annie. And with a sharp movement, that made him wince, she turned his face to her.

'Do you hear?' she repeated, shaking him.

But he was quite dumb. She fetched him a sharp slap on the face. He started, and his eyes widened. Then his face darkened with defiance, after all.

'Do you hear?' she repeated.

He only looked at her with hostile eyes.

'Speak!' she said, putting her face devilishly near his.

'What?' he said, almost overcome.

'You've got to *choose*!' she cried, as if it were some terrible menace, and as if it hurt her that she could not exact more.

'What?' he said, in fear.

'Choose your girl, Coddy. You've got to choose her now. And you'll get your neck broken if you play any more of your tricks, my boy. You're settled now.'

There was a pause. Again he averted his face. He was cunning in his overthrow. He did not give in to them really – no, not if they tore him to bits.

'All right then,' he said, 'I choose Annie.' His voice was strange and full of malice. Annie let go of him as if he had been a hot coal.

'He's chosen Annie!' said the girls in chorus.

'Me!' cried Annie. She was still kneeling, but away from him. He was still lying prostrate, with averted face. The girls grouped uneasily around.

'Me!' repeated Annie, with a terrible bitter accent.

Then she got up, drawing away from him with strange disgust and bitterness.

'I wouldn't touch him,' she said.

But her face quivered with a kind of agony, she seemed as if she would fall. The other girls turned aside. He remained lying on the floor, with his torn clothes and bleeding, averted face.

'Oh, if he's chosen –' said Polly.

'I don't want him – he can choose again,' said Annie, with the same rather bitter hopelessness.

'Get up,' said Polly, lifting his shoulder. 'Get up.'

He rose slowly, a strange, ragged dazed creature. The girls eyed him from a distance, curiously, furtively, dangerously.

'Who wants him?' cried Laura roughly.

'Nobody,' they answered, with contempt. Yet each one of them waited for him to look at her, hoped he would look at her. All except Annie, and something was broken in her.

He, however, kept his face closed and averted from them all. There was a silence of the end. He picked up the torn pieces of his tunic, without knowing what to do with them. The girls stood about uneasily, flushed, panting, tidying their hair and their dress unconsciously, and watching him. He looked at none of them. He espied his cap in a corner, and went and picked it up. He put it on his head, and one of the girls burst into a shrill, hysteric laugh at the sight he presented. He, however, took no heed, but went straight over to where his overcoat hung on a peg. The girls moved away from contact with him as if he had been an electric wire. He put on his coat and buttoned it down. Then he rolled his tunic-rags into a bundle, and stood before the locked door, dumbly.

'Open the door, somebody,' said Laura.

'Annie's got the key,' said one.

Annie silently offered the key to the girls. Nora unlocked the door.

'Tit for tat, old man,' she said. 'Show yourself a man, and don't bear a grudge.'

But without a word or sign he had opened the door and gone, his face closed, his head dropped.

'That'll learn him,' said Laura.

'Coddy!' said Nora.

'Shut up, for God's sake!' cried Annie fiercely, as if in torture.

'Well, I'm about ready to go, Polly. Look sharp!' said Muriel.

The girls were all anxious to be off. They were tidying themselves hurriedly, with mute, stupefied faces.

Katherine Mansfield

'Miss Brill' (1922)

This complete story was written shortly after Mansfield's second collection *Bliss and Other Stories*. It became one of her best-known, if not one of her best stories.

The story resembles a monologue; it illustrates well the way in which Mansfield experimented with narrative voice. Although told in the third person, the voice of most of the story is clearly that of Miss Brill.

Although it was so brilliantly fine – the blue sky powdered with gold and great spots of light like white wine splashed over the Jardins Publiques –

Miss Brill was glad that she had decided on her fur. The air was motionless, but when you opened your mouth there was just a faint chill, like a chill from a glass of iced water before you sip, and now and again a leaf came drifting – from nowhere, from the sky. Miss Brill put up her hand and touched her fur. Dear little thing! It was nice to feel it again. She had taken it out of its box that afternoon, shaken out the moth-powder, given it a good brush, and rubbed the life back into the dim little eyes. 'What has been happening to me?' said the sad little eyes. Oh, how sweet it was to see them snap at her again from the red eiderdown! … But the nose, which was of some black composition, wasn't at all firm. It must have had a knock, somehow. Never mind – a little dab of black sealing-wax when the time came – when it was absolutely necessary … Little rogue! Yes, she really felt like that about it. Little rogue biting its tail just by her left ear. She could have taken it off and laid it on her lap and stroked it. She felt a tingling in her hands and arms, but that came from walking, she supposed. And when she breathed, something light and sad – no, not sad, exactly – something gentle seemed to move in her bosom.

There were a number of people out this afternoon, far more than last Sunday. And the band sounded louder and gayer. That was because the Season had begun. For although the band played all the year round on Sundays, out of season it was never the same. It was like some one playing with only the family to listen; it didn't care how it played if there weren't any strangers present. Wasn't the conductor wearing a new coat, too? She was sure it was new. He scraped with his foot and flapped his arms like a rooster about to crow, and the bandsmen sitting in the green rotunda blew out their cheeks and glared at the music. Now there came a little 'flutey' bit – very pretty! – a little chain of bright drops. She was sure it would be repeated. It was; she lifted her head and smiled.

Only two people shared her 'special' seat: a fine old man in a velvet coat, his hands clasped over a huge carved walking-stick, and a big old woman, sitting upright, with a roll of knitting on her embroidered apron. They did not speak. This was disappointing, for Miss Brill always looked forward to the conversation. She had become really quite expert, she thought, at listening as though she didn't listen, at sitting in other people's lives just for a minute while they talked round her.

She glanced, sideways, at the old couple. Perhaps they would go soon. Last Sunday, too, hadn't been as interesting as usual. An Englishman and his wife, he wearing a dreadful Panama hat and she button boots. And she'd gone on the whole time about how she ought to wear spectacles; she knew she needed them; but that it was no good getting any; they'd be sure to break and they'd never keep

THE MODERN SHORT STORY

on. And he'd been so patient. He'd suggested everything – gold rims, the kind that curved round your ears, little pads inside the bridge. No, nothing would please her. 'They'll always be sliding down my nose!' Miss Brill had wanted to shake her.

The old people sat on the bench, still as statues. Never mind, there was always the crowd to watch. To and fro, in front of the flower-beds and the band rotunda, the couples and groups paraded, stopped to talk, to greet, to buy a handful of flowers from the old beggar who had his tray fixed to the railings. Little children ran among them, swooping and laughing; little boys with big white silk bows under their chins, little girls, little French dolls, dressed up in velvet and lace. And sometimes a tiny staggerer came suddenly rocking into the open from under the trees, stopped, stared, as suddenly sat down 'flop,' until its small high-stepping mother, like a young hen, rushed scolding to its rescue. Other people sat on the benches and green chairs, but they were nearly always the same, Sunday after Sunday, and – Miss Brill had often noticed – there was something funny about nearly all of them. They were odd, silent, nearly all old, and from the way they stared they looked as though they'd just come from dark little rooms or even – even cupboards!

Behind the rotunda the slender trees with yellow leaves down drooping, and through them just a line of sea, and beyond the blue sky with gold-veined clouds.

Tum-tum-tum tiddle-um! tiddle-um! tum tiddley-um tum ta! blew the band.

Two young girls in red came by and two young soldiers in blue met them, and they laughed and paired and went off arm-in-arm. Two peasant women with funny straw hats passed, gravely, leading beautiful smoke-coloured donkeys. A cold, pale nun hurried by. A beautiful woman came along and dropped her bunch of violets, and a little boy ran after to hand them to her, and she took them and threw them away as if they'd been poisoned. Dear me! Miss Brill didn't know whether to admire that or not! And now an ermine toque and a gentleman in grey met just in front of her. He was tall, stiff, dignified, and she was wearing the ermine toque she'd bought when her hair was yellow. Now everything, her hair, her face, even her eyes, was the same colour as the shabby ermine, and her hand, in its cleaned glove, lifted to dab her lips, was a tiny yellowish paw. Oh, she was so pleased to see him – delighted! She rather thought they were going to meet that afternoon. She described where she'd been – everywhere, here, there, along by the sea. The day was so charming – didn't he agree? And wouldn't he, perhaps? … But he shook his head, lighted a cigarette, slowly breathed a great deep puff into her face, and even while she was still talking and laughing, flicked the match away and walked on. The ermine toque was alone; she smiled more brightly than ever. But even the band seemed to know what she was feeling and played more softly, played tenderly, and the drum beat, 'The Brute! The Brute!' over and over. What would she do? What was going to happen now? But as Miss Brill wondered, the ermine toque turned, raised her hand as though she'd seen some one else, much nicer, just over there, and pattered away. And the band changed again and played more quickly, more gayly than ever, and the old couple on Miss Brill's seat got up and marched away, and such a funny old man with long whiskers hobbled along in time to the music and was nearly knocked over by four girls walking abreast.

Oh, how fascinating it was! How she enjoyed it! How she loved sitting here, watching it all! It was like a play. It was exactly like a play. Who could believe the sky at the back wasn't painted? But it wasn't till a little brown dog trotted on solemn and then slowly trotted off, like a little 'theatre' dog, a little dog that had been drugged, that Miss Brill discovered what it was that made it so exciting. They were all on the stage. They weren't only the audience, not only looking on; they were acting. Even she had a part and came every Sunday. No doubt somebody would have noticed if she hadn't been there; she was part of the performance after all. How strange she'd never thought of it like that before! And yet it explained why she made such a point of starting from home at just the same time each week – so as not to be late for the performance – and it also explained why she had quite a queer, shy feeling at telling her English pupils how she spent her Sunday afternoons. No wonder! Miss Brill nearly laughed out loud. She was on the stage. She thought of the old invalid gentleman to whom she read the newspaper four afternoons a week while he slept in the garden. She had got quite used to the frail head on the cotton pillow, the hollowed eyes, the open mouth and the high pinched nose. If he'd been dead she mightn't have noticed for weeks; she wouldn't have minded. But suddenly he knew he was having the paper read to him by an actress! 'An actress!' The old head lifted; two points of light quivered in the old eyes. 'An actress – are ye?' And Miss Brill smoothed the newspaper as though it were the manuscript of her part and said gently; 'Yes, I have been an actress for a long time.'

The band had been having a rest. Now they started again. And what they played was warm, sunny, yet there was just a faint chill – a something, what was it? – not sadness – no, not sadness – a something that made you want to sing. The tune lifted, lifted, the light shone; and it seemed to Miss Brill that in another moment all of them, all the whole company, would begin singing. The young ones, the laughing ones who were moving together, they would begin, and the men's voices, very resolute and brave, would join them. And then she too, she too, and the others on the benches – they would come in with a kind of accompaniment – something low, that scarcely rose or fell, something so beautiful – moving … And Miss Brill's eyes filled with tears and she looked smiling at all the other members of the company. Yes, we understand, we understand, she thought – though what they understood she didn't know.

Just at that moment a boy and girl came and sat down where the old couple had been. They were beautifully dressed; they were in love. The hero and heroine, of course, just arrived from his father's yacht. And still soundlessly singing, still with that trembling smile, Miss Brill prepared to listen.

'No, not now,' said the girl. 'Not here, I can't.'

'But why? Because of that stupid old thing at the end there?' asked the boy. 'Why does she come here at all – who wants her? Why doesn't she keep her silly old mug at home?'

'It's her fu-ur which is so funny,' giggled the girl. 'It's exactly like a fried whiting.'

'Ah, be off with you!' said the boy in an angry whisper. Then: 'Tell me, ma petite chere–'

'No, not here,' said the girl. 'Not yet.'

*   *   *   *   *   *   *   *

On her way home she usually bought a slice of honey-cake at the baker's. It was her Sunday treat. Sometimes there was an almond in her slice, sometimes not. It made a great difference. If there was an almond it was like carrying home a tiny present – a surprise – something that might very well not have been there. She hurried on the almond Sundays and struck the match for the kettle in quite a dashing way.

But to-day she passed the baker's by, climbed the stairs, went into the little dark room – her room like a cupboard – and sat down on the red eiderdown. She sat there for a long time. The box that the fur came out of was on the bed. She unclasped the necklet quickly; quickly, without looking, laid it inside. But when she put the lid on she thought she heard something crying.

Elizabeth Bowen

From 'Maria' (1934)

'Maria' is the story of an orphan girl who is sent to live with the Doselys for a few weeks. But rather than a sentimental story of an awkward young girl who is 'saved', it is about Maria's attempts to get herself sent home and to ruin the career of Mr Hammond, the curate who lives with the Doselys. It is set some time after the First World War in a middle class context, whilst Maria's connections are decidedly upper class. In the opening scene, Maria sits listening while arrangements are made for her to stay with the Doselys.

'We have girls of our own, you see,' Mrs Dosely said, smiling warmly.

That seemed to settle it. Maria's aunt, Lady Rimlade, relaxed at last in Mrs Dosely's armchair, and glancing round once more at the rectory drawing room's fluttery white curtains, alert-looking photographs, and silver cornets spuming out pink sweet pea, consigned Maria to these pleasant influences.

'Then that will be delightful,' she said in that blandly conclusive tone in which she declared open so many bazaars. 'Thursday next, then, Mrs Dosely, about tea-time?'

'That will be delightful.'

'It is *most* kind,' Lady Rimlade concluded.

Maria could not agree with them. She sat scowling under her hat-brim, tying her gloves into knots. Evidently, she thought, I *am* being paid for.

Maria thought a great deal about money; she had no patience with other people's affectations about it, for she enjoyed being a rich little girl. She was only sorry not to know how much they considered her worth; having been sent out to walk in the garden while her aunt had just a short chat, dear, with the Rector's wife. The first phase of the chat, about her own character, she had been able to follow perfectly as she wound her way in and out of some crescent-shaped lobelia beds under the drawing room window. But just as the two voices changed – one going unconcerned, one very, very diffident – Mrs Dosely approached the window and, with an air of immense unconsciousness, shut it. Maria was balked.

Maria was at one of those comfortable schools where everything is attended to. She was (as she had just heard her Aunt Ena explaining to Mrs Dosely) a motherless girl, sensitive, sometimes difficult, deeply reserved. At school they took all this, with her slight tendency to curvature and her dislike of all puddings, into loving consideration. She was having her character 'done' for her – later on, when she came out, would be time for her hair and complexion. In addition to this, she learnt swimming, dancing, some French, the more innocent aspects of history, and *noblesse oblige*. It was a really nice school. All the same, when Maria came home for the holidays they could not do enough to console her for being a motherless girl who had been sent away.

Then, late last summer term, with inconceivable selfishness, her Uncle Philip fell ill, and, in fact, nearly died. Aunt Ena had written less often and very distractedly, and when Maria came home she was told, with complete disregard for her motherlessness, that her uncle and aunt would be starting at once for a cruise, and that she was 'to be arranged for'.

This was not so easy. All the relations and all the family friends (who declared when Sir Philip was ill they'd do anything in the world), wrote back their deepest disappointment at being unable to have Maria just now, though there was nothing, had things been otherwise, that they would have enjoyed more. One to his farm in fact, said Mr MacRobert, the vicar, when he was consulted, another to his merchandise. Then he suggested his neighbours, a Mr and Mrs Dosely, of Malton Peele. He came over to preach in Lent; Lady Rimlade had met him; he seemed such a nice man, frank, cheerful and earnest. *She* was exceedingly motherly, everyone said, and sometimes took in Indian children to make ends meet. The Doselys would be suitable, Maria's aunt felt at once. When Maria raged, she drew down urbane pink eyelids and said she did wish Maria would not be rude. So she drove Maria and the two little griffons over the next afternoon to call upon Mrs Dosely. If Mrs Dosely really seemed sympathetic, she thought she might leave the two little dogs with her too.

'And Mrs Dosely has girls of her own, she tells me,' said Lady Rimlade on the way home. 'I should not wonder if you made quite friends with them. I should not wonder if it was they who had done the flowers. I thought the flowers were done very nicely; I noticed them. Of course, I do not care myself for small silver vases like that, shaped like cornets, but I thought the effect in the Rectory drawing room very cheerful and homelike.'

Angela Carter

'The Snow Child' (1979)

This complete story is based on a few fairy tale elements: a wish for a beautiful girl; a jealous wife; magical transformations. But the similarity ends there; Carter has added sex and an unexpected ending.

Midwinter – invincible, immaculate. The Count and his wife go riding, he on a grey mare and she on a black one, she wrapped in the glittering pelts of black foxes; and she wore high, black, shining boots with scarlet heels, and spurs. Fresh snow fell on snow already fallen; when it ceased, the whole world was white. 'I wish I had a girl as white as snow,' says the Count. They ride on. They come to a hole in the snow; this hole is filled with blood. He says: 'I wish I had a girl as red as blood.' So they ride on again; here is a raven, perched on a bare bough. 'I wish I had a girl as black as that bird's feather.'

As soon as he completed her description, there she stood, beside the road, white skin, red mouth, black hair and stark naked; she was the child of his desire and the Countess hated her. The Count lifted her up and sat her in front of him on his saddle but the Countess had only one thought: how shall I be rid of her?

The Countess dropped her glove in the snow and told the girl to get down to look for it; she meant to gallop off and leave her there but the Count said: 'I'll buy you new gloves.' At that, the furs sprang off the Countess's shoulders and twined round the naked girl. Then the Countess threw her diamond brooch through the ice of a frozen pond: 'Dive in and fetch it for me,' she said; she thought the girl would drown. But the Count said: 'Is she a fish, to swim in such cold weather?' Now the Countess was bare as a bone and the girl furred and booted; the Count felt sorry for his wife. They came to a bush of roses, all in flower. 'Pick me one,' said the Countess to the girl. 'I can't deny you that,' said the Count.

So the girl picks a rose; pricks her finger on the thorn; bleeds; screams; falls.

Weeping, the Count got off his horse, unfastened his breeches and thrust his virile member into the dead girl. The countess reigned in her stamping mare and watched him narrowly; he was soon finished.

Then the girl began to melt. Soon there was nothing left of her but a feather a bird might have dropped; a bloodstain, like the trace of a fox's kill on the snow; and the rose she had pulled off the bush. Now the Countess had all her clothes on again. With her long hand, she stroked her furs. The Count picked up the rose, bowed and handed it to his wife; when she touched it, she dropped it.

'It bites!' she said.

THE MODERN SHORT STORY

Raymond Carver

From 'Preservation' (1983)

This extract is taken from the end of the story in which a man has been made redundant from work. Told from the wife's point of view, she becomes increasingly worried that he has not moved from the sofa for some time. Then the fridge breaks down, and the wife cooks a meal before setting off to buy a new fridge. The scene is typically urban and bleak but the story might be interpreted in the light of the increased optimism of some of Carver's later stories.

The pan was starting to smoke. She poured in more oil and turned on the fan. She hadn't been to an auction in twenty years, and now she was getting ready to go to one tonight. But first she had to dry these pork chops. It was bad luck their fridge had gone flooey, but she found herself looking forward to this auction. She began missing her dad. She even missed her mom now, though the two of them used to argue all the time before she met her husband and began living with him. She stood at the stove, turning the meat, and missing both her dad and her mom.

Still missing them, she took a pot holder and moved the pan off the stove. Smoke was being drawn up through the vent over the stove. She stepped to the doorway with the pan and looked into the living room. The pan was still smoking and drops of oil and grease jumped over the sides as she held it. In the darkened room, she could just make out her husband's head, and his bare feet. 'Come on out here,' she said. 'It's ready.'

'Okay,' he said.

She saw his head come up from the end of the sofa. She put the pan back on the stove and turned to the cupboard. She took down a couple of plates and put them on the counter. She used her spatula to raise one of the pork chops. Then she lifted it onto a plate. The meat didn't look like meat. It looked like part of an old shoulder blade, or a digging instrument. But she knew it was a pork chop, and she took the other one out of the pan and put that on a plate, too.

In a minute, her husband came into the kitchen. He looked at the fridge once more, which was standing there with its door open. And then his eyes took in the pork chops. His mouth dropped open, but he didn't say anything. She waited for him to say something, anything, but he didn't. She put salt and pepper on the table and told him to sit down.

'Sit down,' she said and gave him a plate on which lay the remains of a pork chop. 'I want you to eat this,' she said. He took the plate.

But he just stood there and looked at it. Then she turned to get her own plate.

Sandy cleared the newspaper away and shoved the food to the far side of the table. 'Sit down,' she said to her husband once more. He moved his plate from one hand to the other. But he kept standing there. It was then she saw puddles of water on the table. She heard water, too. It was dripping off the table and onto the linoleum.

She looked down at her husband's bare feet. She stared at his feet next to the pool of water. She knew she'd never again see anything so unusual. But she didn't know what to make of it yet. She thought she'd better put on some lipstick, get her coat, and go ahead to the auction. But she couldn't take her eyes from her husband's feet. She put her plate on the table and watched until the feet left the kitchen and went back into the living room.

Ann Beattie

'Snow' (1986)

I remember the cold night you bought in a pile of logs and a chipmunk jumped off as you lowered your arms. 'What do you think you're doing in here?' you said, as it ran through the living room. It went through the library and stopped at the front door as though it knew the house well. This would be difficult for anyone to believe, except perhaps as the subject of a poem. Our first week in the house was spent scraping, finding some of the house's secrets, like wallpaper underneath wallpaper. In the kitchen, a pattern of white-gold trellises supported purple grapes as big and round as Ping-Pong balls. When we painted the walls yellow, I thought of the bits of grape that remained underneath and imagined the vine popping through, the way some plants can tenaciously push through anything. The day of the big snow, when you had to shovel the walk and couldn't find your cap and asked me how to wind a towel so that it would stay on your head – you, in the white towel turban, like a crazy king of snow. People liked the idea of our being together, leaving the city for the country. So many people visited, and the fireplace made all of them want to tell amazing stories: the child who happened to be standing on the right corner when the door of the ice-cream truck came open and hundreds of Popsicles crashed out; the man standing on the beach, sand sparkling in the sun, one bit glinting more than the rest, stooping to find a diamond ring. Did they talk about amazing things because they thought we'd turn into one of them? Now I think they probably guessed it wouldn't work. It was as hopeless as giving a child a matched cup and saucer. Remember the night, out on the lawn, knee-deep in snow, chins pointed at the sky as the wind whirled down all that whiteness? It seemed that the world had been turned upside down, and we were looking into an enormous field of Queen Anne's lace. Later, headlights off, our car was the first to ride through the newly fallen snow. The world outside the car looked solarized.

You remember it differently. You remember that the cold settled in stages, that a small curve of light was shaved from the moon night after night, until you were no longer surprised the sky was black, that the chipmunk ran to hide in the dark, not simply to a door that led to its escape. Our visitors told the same stories people always tell. One night, giving me a lesson in storytelling, you said, 'Any life will seem dramatic if you omit mention of most of it.'

This, then, for drama: I drove back to that house not long ago. It was April, and Allen had died. In spite of all the visitors, Allen, next door, had been the good friend in bad times. I sat with his wife in their living room, looking out the glass doors to the backyard, and there was Allen's pool, still covered with black plastic that had been stretched across it for the winter. It had rained, and as the rain fell, the cover collected more and more water until it finally spilled onto the concrete. When I left that day, I drove past what had been our house. Three or four crocuses were blooming in the front – just a few dots of white, no field of snow. I felt embarrassed for them. They couldn't compete.

This is a story, told the way you say stories should be told: Somebody grew up, fell in love, and spent a winter with her lover in the country. This, of course, is the barest outline, and futile to discuss. It's as pointless as throwing birdseed on the ground while snow still falls fast. Who expects small things to survive when even the largest get lost? People forget years and remember moments. Seconds and symbols are left to sum things up: the black shroud over the pool. Love, in its shortest form, becomes a word. What I remember about all that time is one winter. The snow. Even now, saying 'snow,' my lips move so that they kiss the air.

No mention has been made of the snowplow that seemed always to be there, scraping snow off our narrow road – an artery cleared, though neither of us could have said where the heart was.

Nadine Gordimer

'Once Upon A Time' (1991)

Set in apartheid South Africa, probably towards the end of that era, a writer tells herself a bedtime story to help her get to sleep. The story tells of a middle class white family who go further and further with their home security until, finally, the consequences are disastrous.

Someone has written to ask me to contribute to an anthology of stories for children. I reply that I don't write children's stories: and he writes back that at a recent congress/book fair/seminar a certain novelist said every writer ought to write at least one story for children. I think of sending a postcard saying I don't accept that I 'ought' to write anything.

And then last night I woke up – or rather was awakened without knowing what had aroused me.

A voice in the echo-chamber of the subconscious?

A sound.

A creaking of the kind made by the weight carried by one foot after another along a wooden floor. I listened. I felt the apertures of my ears distend with concentration. Again: the creaking. I was waiting for it: waiting to hear if it indicated that feet were moving from room to room, coming up the passage – to my door. I have no burglar bars, no gun under the pillow. But I have the same fears as people who take these precautions, and my windowpanes are thin as rime. Could shatter like a wineglass. A woman was murdered (how do they put it) in broad daylight in a house two blocks away. Last year, and the fierce dogs who guarded an old widower and his collection of antique clocks were strangled before he was knifed by a casual labourer he had dismissed without pay.

I was staring at the door, making it out in my mind rather than seeing it, in the dark. I lay quite still – a victim already – but the arrhythmia of my heart was fleeing, knocking this way and that against its body cage. How finely tuned the senses are, just out of rest, sleep! I could never listen intently as that in the distractions of the day; I was reading every faintest sound, identifying and classifying its possible threat.

But I learned that I was to be neither threatened nor spared. There was no human weight pressing on the boards, the creaking was a buckling, an epicentre of stress. I was in it. The house that surrounds me while I sleep is built on undermined ground: far beneath my bed, the floor, the house's foundations, the stopes and passages of gold mines have hollowed the rock, and when some face trembles, detaches and falls, three thousand feet below, the whole house shifts slightly, bringing uneasy strain to the balance and counterbalance of brick, cement, wood and glass that hold it as a structure around me. The misbeats of my heart tailed off like the last muffled flourishes on one of the wooden xylophones made by the Chopi and Tsonga migrant miners who might have been down there, under me in the earth at that moment. The stope where the fall was could have been disused, dripping water from its ruptured veins: or men might now be interred there in the most profound of tombs.

I couldn't find a position in which my mind would let go of my body – release me to sleep again. So I began to tell myself a story: a bedtime story.

In a house, in a suburb, in a city there were a man and a wife who loved each other very much and were living happily ever after. They had a little boy, and they loved him very much. They had a cat and a dog that the little boy loved very much. They had a car and a caravan trailer for holidays, and a swimming-pool which was fenced so that the little boy and his playmates would not fall in and drown. They had a housemaid who was absolutely trustworthy and an itinerant gardener who was highly recommended by the neighbours. For when they began to live happily ever after they were warned by that wise old witch, the husband's mother, not to take on anyone off the street. They were inscribed in a medical benefit society, their pet dog was licensed, they were insured against fire, flood damage and theft, and subscribed to the local Neighbourhood Watch, which supplied them with a plaque for their gates lettered YOU HAVE BEEN WARNED over the silhouette of a would-be intruder. He was masked: it could not be said if he was black or white, and therefore proved the property owner was no racist.

It was not possible to insure the house, the swimming pool or the car against riot damage. There were riots, but these were outside the city, where people of another colour were quartered. These people were not allowed into the suburb except as reliable housemaids and gardeners, so there was nothing to fear, the husband told the wife. Yet she was afraid that some day such people might come up the street and tear off the plaque YOU HAVE BEEN WARNED and open the gate and stream in … Nonsense, my dear, said the husband, there are police and soldiers and tear-gas and guns to keep them away. But to please her – for he loved her very much and buses were being burned, cars stoned, and schoolchildren shot by the police in those quarters out of sight and hearing of the suburb – he had electronically-controlled gates fitted. Anyone who pulled off the sign

YOU HAVE BEEN WARNED and tried to open the gates would have to announce his intentions by pressing a button and speaking into a receiver relayed to the house. The little boy was fascinated by the device and used it as a walkie-talkie in cops and robbers play with his small friends.

The riots were suppressed, but there were many burglaries in the suburb and somebody's trusted housemaid was tied up and shut in a cupboard by thieves while she was in charge of her employer's house. The trusted housemaid of the man and wife and little boy was so upset by this misfortune befalling a friend left, as she herself often was, with responsibility for the possessions of the man and his wife and the little boy that she implored her employers to have burglar bars attached to the doors and windows of the house, and an alarm system installed. The wife said, She is right, let us take heed of her advice. So from every window and door in the house where they were living happily ever after they now saw the trees and sky through bars, and when the little boy's pet cat tried to climb in by the fanlight to keep him company in his little bed at night, as it customarily had done, it set off the alarm keening through the house.

The alarm was often answered – it seemed – by other burglar alarms, in other houses, that had been triggered by pet cats or nibbling mice. The alarms called to one another across the garden in shrills and bleats and wails that everyone soon became accustomed to, so that the din roused the inhabitants of the suburb no more than the croak of frogs and musical grating of cicadas' legs. Under cover of the electronic harpies' discourse intruders sawed the iron bars and broke into homes, taking away hi-fi equipment, television sets, cassette players, cameras and radios, jewellery and clothing, and sometimes were hungry enough to devour everything in the refrigerator or paused audaciously to drink the whisky in the cabinets or patio bars. Insurance companies paid no compensation for single malt, a loss made keener by the property owner's knowledge that the thieves wouldn't even have been able to appreciate what it was they were drinking.

Then time came when many of the people who were not trusted housemaids and gardeners hung about the suburb because they were unemployed. Some importuned for a job: weeding or painting a roof: anything, *bass*, madam. But the man and his wife remembered the warning about taking on anyone off the street. Some drank liquor and fouled the street with discarded bottles. Some begged, waiting for the man or his wife to drive the car out of the electronically-operated gates. They sat about with their feet in the gutters, under the jacaranda trees that made a green tunnel of the street – for it was a beautiful suburb, spoilt only by their presence – and sometimes they fell asleep lying right before the gates in the midday sun. The wife could never see anyone go hungry. She sent the trusted housemaid out with bread and tea, but the trusted housemaid said these were loafers and *tsotsis*, who would come and tie her up and shut her in a cupboard. The husband said, She's right. Take heed of her advice. You only encourage them with your bread and tea. They are looking for their chance ... And he brought the little boy's tricycle from the garden into the house every night, because if the house was surely secure, once locked and with the alarm set, someone might still be able to climb over the wall or the electronically-closed gates into the garden.

You are right, said the wife, then the wall should be higher. And the wise old witch, the husband's mother, paid for the extra bricks as her Christmas present to her son and his wife – the little boy got a Space Man outfit and a book of fairy tales.

But every week there were more reports of intrusion: in broad daylight and the dead of night, in the early hours of the morning, and even in the lovely summer twilight – a certain family was at dinner while the bedrooms were being ransacked upstairs. The man and his wife, talking of the latest armed robbery in the suburbs, were distracted by the sight of the little boy's pet cat effortlessly arriving over the seven-foot wall, descending first with a rapid bracing of extended forepaws down on the sheer vertical surface, and then a graceful launch, landing with swishing tail within the property. The whitewashed wall was marked with the cat's coming and goings; and on the street side of the wall there were larger red-earth smudges that could have been made by the kind of broken running shoes, seen on the feet of unemployed loiterers, that had no innocent destination.

When the man and wife and little boy took the pet dog for its walk round the neighbourhood streets they no longer paused to admire the show of roses or that perfect lawn: these were hidden behind an array of different varieties of security fences, walls and devices. The man, wife, little boy and dog passed a remarkable choice: there was the low-cost option of pieces of broken glass embedded in cement along the top of walls, there were iron grills ending in lance-points, there were attempts at reconciling the aesthetics of prison architecture with the Spanish Villa style (spikes painted pink) and with the plaster urns of neo-classical façades (twelve-inch pikes finned like zigzags of lightning and painted pure white). Some walls had a small board affixed, giving the name and telephone number of the firm responsible for the installation of the devices. While the little boy and the pet dog raced ahead, the husband and wife found themselves comparing the possible effectiveness of each style against its appearance; and after several weeks when they paused before this barricade or that without needing to speak, both came out with the conclusion that only one was worth considering. It was the ugliest but the most honest in its suggestion of the pure concentration-camp style, no frills, all evident efficacy. Placed the length of walls, it consisted of a continuous coil of stiff and shining metal serrated into jagged edges, so that there would be no way of climbing over it and no way through its tunnel without getting entangled in its fangs. There would be no way out, only a struggle getting bloodier and bloodier, a deeper and sharper hooking and tearing of flesh. The wife shuddered to look at it. You're right, said the husband, anyone would think twice … And they took heed of the advice on a small board fixed to the wall: Consult DRAGON's TEETH The People For Total Security.

Next day a gang of workmen came and stretched the razor-bladed coils all round the walls of the house where the husband and wife and little boy and pet dog and cat were living happily ever after. The sunlight flashed and slashed, off the serrations, the cornice of razor thorns encircled the home, shining. The husband said, Never mind. It will weather. The wife said, You're wrong. They guaranteed it's rust-proof. And she waited until the little boy had run off to play before she said, I hope the cat will take heed … the husband said, Don't worry, my dear, cats always look before they leap. And it was true that from that day on the cat slept in the little boy's bed and kept to the garden, never risking a try at breaching security.

One evening, the mother read the little boy to sleep with a fairy story from the book the wise old witch had given him at Christmas. Next day he pretended to be the Prince who braves the terrible thicket of thorns to enter the palace and kiss the Sleeping Beauty back to life: he dragged a ladder to the wall, the shining coiled tunnel was just wide enough for his little body to creep in, and with the first fixing of its razor-teeth in his knees and hands and head he screamed and struggled deeper into its tangle. The trusted housemaid and the itinerant gardener, whose 'day' it was, came running, the first to see and to scream with him, and the itinerant gardener tore his hands trying to get to the little boy. Then the man and his wife burst wildly into the garden and for some reason (the cat, probably) the alarm set up wailing against the screams while the bleeding mass of the little boy was hacked out of the security coil with saws, wire cutters, choppers, and they carried it – the man, the wife, the hysterical trusted housemaid and the weeping gardener – into the house.

Sources of the beginnings

The beginnings on pages 71–73 are taken from the following short stories and novels:

Extract 1: Charles Dickens *Great Expectations* (1860–1861) – novel

Extract 2: Thomas Hardy 'The Melancholy Hussar of the German Legion' (1889) – short story

Extract 3: Edgar Allan Poe 'The Cask of Amontillado' (1846) – short story

Extract 4: Roger Mais 'Red Dirt Don't Wash' (1986) – short story

Extract 5: Robert Louis Stevenson 'Markheim' (1885) – short story

Extract 6: Jamaica Kincaid 'My Mother' (1984) – short story

Extract 7: Thomas Hardy *The Mayor of Casterbridge* (1886) – novel

4 | Critical approaches

- How have writers and critics attempted to explain short stories?

- How useful are these approaches for interpreting individual stories?

- Do short stories require different methods of interpretation from other genres, such as novels?

- How have critical views of the short story changed?

Part 4 introduces the main theoretical approaches to the study of short stories. The approaches are divided into structural approaches, thematic approaches and reader-oriented approaches. It is not the purpose of this part to offer detailed interpretations of the stories referred to in this book.

Short stories share many features with the novel such as narrative (story telling, characterisation, point of view) and so the novel is an obvious point of comparison. However, it is worth paying attention to the special features of short stories that critics have discovered, some of which were described in Part 2. These features may help in understanding the way that individual stories work, but the stories can also be used to test the theories that critics have proposed. It works both ways: theory can explain story or story can test theory. Both of these depend on you, the reader and your willingness to read critically. Part 4 shows how to read short stories using critical approaches, but also how to read the critics using the stories.

The metaphors' game

The way that critics approach a literary work is often underpinned by a basic metaphor. So, for example, some critics consider the novel to be like a journey that the reader and some of the characters undertake. A particular novel might be like a journey because the main character takes many wrong turnings before eventually finding the right path – a journey of self-discovery (for example, Jane Austen's *Emma*). What then is the best metaphor for short stories? For example, Chekhov described his writing as 'lacy' in the sense that he left out so much that the holes in his stories were more substantial than the cloth. This also picks up on the idea that the word 'text' is related to 'textile' which suggests words woven together to make a complete story.

▶ Before reading on, consider in what ways the short story is like the following: a snapshot, modelling a sphere out of clay, a cook turning out a blancmange, an iceberg, evidence for a detective, a sentence.

Which of these metaphors best sums up your experience of short stories?

Poe's theory of the modern short story

The first 'theory' of the modern short story was undoubtedly Poe's. Poe believed that the short story was a superior form to the novel because it could be taken in at a single sitting. This helped to create what he saw as its major artistic feature – its 'unity of impression'. In other words, everything in the story should be aimed at enhancing or reinforcing a single idea and there should be no redundant words. For Poe, this unity was achieved through the author's 'preconceived effect', as if everything the author intended about his or her literary work could be transplanted unscathed inside the mind of the reader. In 'The Fall of the House of Usher' (1840), for example, the effect was one of utter spiritual and physical decay. Later critics have strongly challenged this idea, suggesting that the reader plays an equally important part in the creation of meaning. It should also be borne in mind that Poe's views were motivated both by his ambitions to promote his own magazine, and by the nationalistic urges of American writers at the time to establish an American literature that was independent of Europe.

In Poe's own work it is easy to see that his stories create an intense impression of, for example, what it is like to be entombed in a dungeon. In the work of 20th-century writers such as Carver or Munro, the unity of impression centres on concepts such as 'the gulf between mothers and their daughters', 'growing up', or 'desperate relationships in the urban world'. Poe's 'unity' might be divided into two related ideas: first, the familiar notion that interpretation traditionally involves relating as much of the story as possible to a central 'theme'; second, in stories with strong plots, the idea that everything has been leading up to the final twist at the end of the story, as for example in Maupassant's famous story 'The Necklace'. However, in connection with the first of these, Poe's idea of unity is not exactly the same as theme: unity encompassed an intense emotion and atmosphere rather than an intellectual unifying of ideas in the story.

Story shapes and structural approaches

Structural approaches tend to break stories down into their constituent parts, often summarising the relationship between these parts by means of a diagram. Such diagrams were beloved of the short story manuals that proliferated in the 1920s and were later given more credibility by **structuralist critics**. These critics used language as the model for understanding stories and attempted to show how stories could be broken down into interconnected parts. However, these approaches are in fact ancient, as well as comparatively new. In ancient Greece, Aristotle provided the most basic structure of a beginning, a middle and an end, but then, using this theory, how do we distinguish between a story and a piece of string? The theory is too general to be of much use. Interestingly, with respect to Aristotle, one of Chekhov's famous pieces of advice about writing short stories was that writers should write their story and then delete the beginning and the end. Here Chekhov raises the crucial issue of what is left out of short stories, which is important for considering what the reader provides.

The German critic, Gustav Freytag, used an inverted V shape to describe the structure of stories, including novels and plays, rather than modern short stories as such. The structure is: (a) exposition (see page 61); (b) development of the conflict; (c) the conflict, and (d) the resolution of the conflict. However, this shape does not apply to most of the stories mentioned in this book, with the exception of some by the more traditional 19th-century writers such as Hardy and Dickens, and a little later, H.G. Wells. Today short stories may work by deliberately denying this kind of conventional structure, especially if the reader is expecting it. This has become particularly apparent in the last few decades as the trend has moved towards both minimalism and ambiguous endings.

How many events does it take to make a story? Many critics take the minimum number to be three, perhaps because of Aristotle's beginning, middle and end, or perhaps because there is simply something aesthetically pleasing about the number three in literary contexts. However, in keeping with this tendency towards omission, some have reduced short stories to a simple two-part structure. Certainly the latter could be applied to Poe, many of whose stories were of the structure: person in predicament – person gets out of predicament, or problem – solution. Similarly but in a completely different context, James Joyce's 'Eveline' (1913) is the story of a woman who wants to run away with a man but changes her mind at the last minute, thus creating a simple two-part structure.

The structural approach can appear to be rather crude and sterile: so what if a story has five parts? the reader might ask. But the point is not so much how many parts a story has, but the thematic implications of its fitting or not fitting a particular structure. What, in other words, is left out for readers to imagine and how are they to do this? Structures can also help in making comparisons between stories; for example, if a story misses out one part or puts emphasis on another, this may tell the reader something about the way that this particular story works that is different from another. For example, when Raymond Carver rewrote 'The Bath' as 'A Small Good Thing', what part did he think he was adding and what did he originally omit?

▶ Apply one of the above structural approaches to 'Miss Brill' or to 'The Snow Child' (Part 3, pages 83–87 and pages 89–90).

Thematic approaches

Thematic approaches to the short story generally claim that all short stories have some similarity of theme. Given the vast range of subjects available to writers, this means that the similarity must be at a high level of abstraction if it is to be relevant to all possible subjects. Some theories in this category have also been applied to short story writers themselves and their situation.

It can be argued that Poe's views were the first thematic approach to short stories. After all, he emphasised the need to focus on a single idea. This was later taken up by the critic Brander Mathews in 1901 who developed Poe's ideas into a dogma (see Assignment 4 on page 110). Poe's theory is too simple to be of much use today, but arguably it has formed the basis for the more applicable ideas, most of which build on the idea of a single impression.

Epiphany

Epiphany, and indeed modern short stories, have their roots in the ideas of the Romantic poets of the early 19th century. Wordsworth in particular wrote about 'spots of time' – significant moments when some insight was achieved. But, in keeping with the pessimism of the times, more recent versions of epiphany have expressed people's inability to gain insight.

Epiphany literally means 'showing' but its original biblical connotations (see page 32) have long since disappeared as the term has become familiar to readers of the short story. In this context, the term was introduced by James Joyce at the time he was writing the stories for *Dubliners*. It refers to stories in which something important is revealed – a critical moment in a character's life. The important question is: what is revealed to whom and to what purpose? This is where the individual writer's interpretation of 'epiphany' comes into play, and there is more than one possible answer.

The first is where the main character makes a discovery about himself or herself because of the situation that the story has found the character in. 'Situation' – which for many critics is the essence of the short story – refers to a combination of time, events, people and place, and is necessarily shortlived. The implication of this discovery is that psychologically the character will never be the same again as a result of the insight. This type of epiphany lends itself well to situations that mark the changes of life. Thus the changes that occur during childhood, especially during adolescence, are a frequent theme. For example, Susan Hill's 'The Badness Within Him' in *A Bit of Singing and Dancing* (1973), ends with weeping as Col realises that 'his childhood had ended too'.

The second variation on the epiphany theme is where the revelation is only for the reader, with the implication that the character in question remains oblivious to the change or to the potential change. Notice that the character may have changed but not be aware of it or they may not have changed at all. In the latter cases, the epiphany is charged with irony, with the reader perhaps pitying the character for their lack of insight. This kind of epiphany became typical of 20th-century writing with its bleak and ironic vision of human nature.

In many stories the nature of the epiphany is ambiguous. Epiphany as an idea certainly helps to explain many stories, but it also retains a sense of something unknown. For example, Graham Greene's 'I Spy'(1930) is about a boy who sneaks downstairs at night to steal from his father's shop. He finds his father there about to be taken away by two men, presumably for spying (the events of the story take place during the First World War). The story ends like this:

> When the door had closed Charlie Stowe tiptoed upstairs and got into bed. He wondered why his father had left the house again so late at night and who the strangers were. Surprise and awe kept him for a little while awake. It was as if a familiar photograph had stepped from the frame to reproach him with neglect. He remembered how his father had held tight to his collar and fortified himself with proverbs, and he thought for the first time that, while his mother was boisterous and kindly, his father was very like himself, doing things in the dark which frightened him. It would have pleased him to go down to his father and tell him that he loved him, but he could hear through the window the quick steps going away. He was alone in the house with his mother, and he fell asleep.

Clearly the boy has learned something about his relationship with his father and the story could be interpreted as being about a boy identifying with his father as he grows up. The action is seen entirely through the boy's eyes so the uncertainties are his ('He wondered …', 'it was as if …'). He seems remarkably clear about other things, like the comparison between his father and his mother. But these certainties seem to be undermined by the reader's superior position – the reader by now has a good idea of what is happening to the father – can Charlie Stowe really be fully aware of the psychological importance of what has happened? Even if Charlie's insight is as clear as some of the text implies, his emotions are still left unfulfilled as he is unable to say goodbye to his father and is 'alone' with his mother. There are hints of a seed of awareness sown rather than full-blown revelation.

This epiphany, then, is blurred and the reader might wonder if Greene has succeeded in concealing enough from his naive young character, whilst revealing enough understanding to his readers. What also becomes apparent about epiphany is that although a story might revolve around a single moment, such as this one, the moment itself is crowded with a plethora of mixed feelings, memories and comparisons. The identification of an epiphany within a story can seem a simplistic way of reading critically, but this is clearly not so: epiphanies might be better seen as a kind of crossroads for human experience – that is, significant in themselves but informed and influenced by a wide range of emotions from elsewhere in the story.

Below are three interpretations of Katherine Mansfield's 'Miss Brill', using the epiphany theory. They illustrate that 'epiphany' as a theoretical tool for analysing stories provides a starting point, but not an automatic answer to critical problems.

> The ending is sometimes objected to on the grounds of its sentimentality which obscures the revelation that has been offered to Miss Brill in the park ... Since Miss Brill is the single focalizer [the story is told only from her point of view], the closing anthropomorphic perception – the imagined crying of the fur – is clearly another example of the character's self-delusion, which persists, but in a state of crisis: a revelation of self-awareness has been offered, and now Miss Brill struggles to efface this insight. The conclusion comprises a complex, ambivalent epiphany which emulates the character's own internal conflict between awareness and delusion, and this confusion is the essence of Miss Brill's condition.
>
> (Dominic Head *The Modernist Short Story*, 1992)

> The Crushing rebuff she receives is evidently accidental, but the minute episodes somehow appear to be sequential or related as cause and effect. Her every perception contributes to her emotional state and in some fashion promises her happiness, yet makes probable her final misery ... at the end, even inanimate objects have the power to make her unhappy; she has been permanently relegated to the 'dark little rooms or even – cupboards'.
>
> (Theodore Stroud in *Short Story Theories*, ed. Charles May, 1976)

> Although many readers by this almost midpoint of the story may have begun to look askance at Miss Brill herself, the full effect of her observation of the others does not come until she goes home, her day ruined by a young woman's saying that her fox fur looks like 'a fried whiting'. Miss Brill is so hurt that she does not even stop at the baker's to get her usual 'slice of honey-cake,' which sometimes has an almond in it. Tenderly demonstrating in what small ways a person may make her own life ever so slightly pleasant, Mansfield writes that the almond was to Miss Brill 'something that might very well not have been there'. Today without a slice of cake, she climbs the stairs to 'the little dark room – her room like a cupboard'. Mansfield's

handling clearly shows that Miss Brill has never before seen herself as being one of those funny old people. When she returns her fur to its box and puts on the lid, she thinks she hears something crying. Miss Brill herself, like Ma Parker, never has the good cry she so much deserves.

(J.F. Kobler *Katherine Mansfield: A Study of the Short Fiction*, 1990)

▶ By reading the story on pages 83–87 and the three analyses of the ending closely, decide which of them best captures the nature of the epiphany.

Frank O'Connor: outsiders and the 'frontier' experience

The Lonely Voice, written in 1962 by Frank O'Connor, has become one of the most enduring and respected critical analyses of the modern short story. O'Connor's first claim was that short stories represent outsiders in society, both in the sense that stories are about outsiders and the writers themselves are outsiders. His starting point for the argument was Gogol's 'The Overcoat', about an insignificant clerk who wants to get his coat repaired. For O'Connor, this story was one of the first to be about insignificant people – and since then the short story has become adept at dealing with such 'outsiders'. Of course, outsiders are not always economic or political outsiders in the sense of being poor or cast out for their beliefs. There are many other possibilities and these are essential if this view is to have wide applicability. O'Connor called his outsiders 'submerged population groups', although it was a term he did not particularly like.

Here are some examples of stories that suggest loneliness, isolation and outsiders: a woman who is too busy to attend to her own feelings (Janet Frame 'You Are Now Entering the Human Heart', 1984); a woman who is bored with her husband and who wants to stroke a cat (Hemingway 'Cat in the Rain', 1928); three men who are adrift in a small boat after a shipwreck (Stephen Crane 'The Open Boat', 1897).

O'Connor's claim that writers themselves represent submerged population groups has some supporting evidence but is difficult to sustain. The image of the artist in exile is a familiar one and is exemplified by writers as far apart as Hemingway, Somerset Maugham and Samuel Selvon, or even by Raymond Carver in that he was exiled by poverty. O'Connor also applied this idea to whole nations. For him the nations that excelled at short stories were relatively undeveloped (19th-century America) or on the fringes of another great power (Ireland). Although it is not difficult to find counter-examples to the above (for example, France and Russia), there is a plausibility in O'Connor's argument that the transfer of writers' feelings from their own situation to the subject matter of their stories explains why so many short stories dwell on the outsider theme. However, it should be noted that O'Connor does not claim that only Inuits and Native Americans will be able to write short stories in the future: there are enough outsiders already in our midst.

Anticipating much of the writing of the late 20th century, O'Connor felt that short stories are essentially about human loneliness and isolation, hence the title of his book. This view has been supported by many other writers and critics who feel that the form of the short story is particularly suited to the age in which we live. For example, Nadine Gordimer believes that the short story is 'the art of the only thing one can be sure of – the present moment' (in *Kenyon Review*, 1968). She meant by this that the old certainties of 19th-century Britain (see page 26) no longer apply. Religion has lost its force, relationships within marriage are unstable, even the past is open to interpretation and the future is often seen to offer little hope.

A further feature of short stories according to O'Connor is the '**frontier**' experience. This involves a character coming up against a situation that is in some way new. The 'frontier' is really another metaphor for what characters go through in short stories. It refers to the change from one state to another, or life's crossing points, as for example in:

life – death
sanity – insanity
childhood – adulthood
isolation – acceptance into the group/conformity
ignorance – self-knowledge
emotional stasis – catharsis

In some sense the character will move between these states, or will sometimes fail to make it to the other side. It might be argued that there are distinct similarities between this theory and epiphany theory: the epiphany itself is simply the transition from one state to the other. But this oversimplifies. For example, in Faulkner's 'A Rose for Emily' (1931) Emily sleeps with the corpse of her lover as this is the only way that she can keep him. As a frontier, her transition from life to death symbolises her futile clinging to the traditions of the old South. The frontier between her and her acceptance by the community in which she lives is one that she fails to cross. The two frontiers work together to maintain her status as an outsider. Epiphany theory, on the other hand, struggles to explain the complexities of this story. In short, frontier theory offers more variation and seems to account for a wider range of stories, in part because of the metaphorical nature of the 'frontier'.

The great advantage of this theory is that it often allows readers to draw together several stories under the same umbrella; a surprising number of stories have at least some connection with it. However, the danger of a theory like this is that it tries to reduce short stories to a simple formula; one might say that frontier theory, structural theories and epiphany theory are all **reductionist** in their approach. It can be argued that each story has its own individual power that goes beyond the two or three elements of a theory or formula. Rather like a template that can be put over the story to highlight its basic shape, with these approaches something is always lost.

Reader-oriented approaches

In all literary genres the last few decades have seen more emphasis on the role of readers and the context of reading. These approaches examine who the readers are (as in the case of feminism) and the part they play in moving from text to interpretation. This section will briefly sample some of these approaches as they apply to modern short stories.

Reader-oriented approaches can also be seen to have started with Poe because of the emphasis he put on unity of impression as communicated during a single sitting. But since the beginning of the 20th century, many short stories have seemed to defy unity, especially the fragmented works of the post-modernists; the story 'Snow' on pages 92–93 exemplifies this. By using omission and even more radical fragmentation, these writers seemed to be acknowledging that texts do not fix their own meaning, as implied by Poe, but await the contribution of a reader. And because readers come in all shapes and sizes and from a wide range of contexts, the number of possible interpretations has multiplied. So it is now possible to ask questions such as: how would this story be read by a woman? by someone in a colonial context? by a representative of a minority group? Even the more recent theories that seem to unify a story around a central idea such as epiphany have been subjected to fragmentation. Critics such as Dominic Head believe that epiphany as a simple moment of insight is not useful, and that epiphany depends on the reader bringing together varied and contradictory information that finally reveals a complex inner life for the characters in short stories.

▶ Read the story 'Snow' in Part 3. List the ways in which it is fragmented. Do you feel that it is possible for a reader to pull together these fragments into a satisfying reading of the story?

Feminist perspectives

There appears to be no commonly accepted feminist perspective on the modern short story as a form. Margaret Atwood's statement below suggests why there ought to be one:

Women writers belong together because they are different from men, and the writing they do is different as well and cannot be read with the same eyeglasses as those used for the reading of male writers. Nor can writing by women be read in the same way by men as it can by women, and vice versa. For many women, Heathcliff is a romantic hero; for many men, he's a posturing oaf they'd like to punch in the nose. *Paradise Lost* reads differently when read by the daughters of Eve, and with Milton's browbeaten secretarial daughters in mind; and so on down through the canon.

(Women Writers at Work, 1998)

Why should short stories be any different? It could be argued that right from its inception the short story was established on male terms. The idea of significant moments in a life comes from Wordsworth, the single effect from Poe, epiphany from Joyce, and so forth. There have, of course, been important writers of the short story who are women, but you could argue that many of them broke away from the conventional form: Virginia Woolf, who was highly experimental; Angela Carter, who invented a new form in her subverted fairy tales; Alice Munro, whose scale and richness seem to defy the muscular brevity of the pattern laid down by Hemingway and Carver.

There are many questions to ask about the stories themselves. It is possible to read any individual writer from a feminist perspective, as with any other genre, but ideally these readings need to be linked with the perspective on short stories offered in this part of the book. For example, how have women writers used epiphany and what frontiers have they explored? Katherine Mansfield was heavily criticised for leaving her ageing female characters without insight, but to what extent does this reflect a 20th-century trend rather than an attitude towards women? Epiphanies might also be different for male and female characters. For example, Hemingway's Nick 'felt quite sure that he would never die' in 'Indian Camp' (1926), but Janet Frame's narrator in 'You Are Now Entering the Human Heart' (1984) feels that 'The journey through the human heart would have to wait for another time'. Both characters have had disturbing experiences, but they react very differently. An extension of this argument is that if failed epiphanies have become the norm, does that not make women a more suitable subject for epiphanies than men in late 20th-century short stories? Similarly, one could question the role of women in men's frontier experiences. Do they, for example, play a nurturing role, a provocative role, or the role of victim?

1   Read as many stories as you can from Anita Desai's collection *Games at Twilight* (Penguin, 1982). Using any of the approaches outlined in Part 4, to what extent do you feel that this example of post-colonial writing uses a familiar form in an unfamiliar context?

2   Some critics feel that short stories have become so fragmented and ambiguous that the idea of unity is not a useful one. Apply 'unity' to any contemporary short stories you are studying and assess its usefulness.

3   Apply the notion of 'unity' to a story with a strong plot and a twist. To what extent do the features in the main body of the story have significance for the twist?

4   In 1901 Brander Matthews refined Poe's ideas by creating a set of rules about the modern short story: 'a single character, a single event, a single emotion, or the series of emotions called forth by a single situation' ('The Philosophy of the Short Story').
    D.H. Lawrence has the reputation of breaking all of these rules in his stories. To what extent do you agree with this and do you feel that Lawrence's stories suffer as a result?
    Apply Matthews' ideas to the complete stories in Part 3.

5   Omission is often thought by critics to play an important part in the stories that make up *Dubliners*. If you are studying *Dubliners*, make a list of which part of Freytag's curve (see page 102) are most frequently missed out of these stories. Consider the effect of this on the themes and readers' responses.

6   Plotted stories with a twist sometimes end with a moment of revelation, for example, Maupassant's 'The Necklace', Kate Chopin's 'The Story of an Hour', H.G. Wells' 'The Stolen Bacillus', and many stories by Saki. To what extent do you consider these endings to be epiphanies in the sense laid down by James Joyce?

7   The end of a relationship makes a suitable subject for short stories because it is a critical moment. Compare 'Pretty Ice' by Mary Robison (in *The Granta Book of the American Short Story*, 1992) with Hemingway's

'The End of Something'. How do these two writers deal with the end of relationships and does either of them use epiphany?

8 Using an anthology of male and female writing, identify stories that use either epiphanies or frontiers. To what extent do you find that male and female characters are treated differently in these stories? Two anthologies by women are: *The Penguin Book of Modern Women's Short Stories*, ed. Susan Hill (1991), and *Close Company – Stories of Mothers and Daughters*, eds. Park and Heaton (1987).

9 Analyse the extracts by Kipling, Lawrence and Carver (Part 3, pages 80–81, 81–83, and 91–92) with respect to gender relationships. What changes do you detect over time and how might these be connected with the context of writing these stories?

10 Suzanne Ferguson has written that the main formal characteristics of the modern novel and the modern short story are the same: (1) limitation and importance of point of view (2) emphasis on presentation of sensation and inner experience (3) omission of elements of the traditional plot (4) increasing reliance on metaphor (5) rejection of chronological time ordering (6) stylistic economy (7) style itself important (based on *Modern Fiction Studies*, Spring 1982). Compare a modern novel with a selection of 20th-century short stories to test this idea.

11 'Miss Brill' is reproduced in Part 3 (pages 83–87). Find what you regard to be the central epiphany. Many critics feel that a weakness of this story is that Mansfield seems to undermine her own epiphany. Do you think that this is a weakness or a strength of the story? Compare this effect with epiphanies in other stories by Mansfield. See Assignment 2, page 116 on epiphanies in general.

Using three or four of the extracts in Part 3 written by both men and women, create a chart showing similarities and differences between women's stories and men's stories. You might look at the presentation of the characters, the nature of any epiphany or frontier, and the overall form of the stories. Is it possible to argue that short stories written by women are distinct from those written by men?

5 | How to write about short stories

- How do you prepare for writing about short stories?

- How do you read in context?

- How can you make use of critics?

Preparing to write about short stories

Most of this book has been about how to write about short stories, but Part 5 offers practical advice. What follows are suggestions for approaching stories, but these do not have to be followed slavishly.

- Don't treat short stories as if they were the same as novels only shorter. For example, don't look for character sketches as a starting point. Read closely within the story itself, but look outside the story towards social, literary and cultural contexts.

- Pay special attention to the end of the story, asking the following questions:
  (a) Is the ending a recognisable type? See Part 2, page 64.) If so, can you connect it with what has gone before? If it is symbolic, does it pick up on symbols used earlier in the story? For example, in Mansfield's 'The Fly' (1922) how does the man's treatment of the fly reflect on his son's death and what does it ultimately say about him and human nature?
  (b) Does the type of ending immediately suggest an era or story style (as covered in Parts 2 and 4), for example, frame, commentary, ironic twist, symbol, oral story, slice of life, tale, epiphany, frontier?
  (c) How do you respond to the end? Is there any obvious emotional or intellectual reaction? Do you feel as if nothing much has happened? Do you feel as if you can't see the point? If your expected ending is not fulfilled ask yourself why the writer might have defied expectations.

- Whatever you find at the end, try applying it to the main body of the story. If a story ends surprisingly with violence, look for hints or possible causes of violence earlier in the story, as for example, in Joyce's 'A Little Cloud' and 'Counterparts' from *Dubliners*.

- Look for a central idea, image or moment around which the story may revolve. For example, Alecia McKenzie's story 'Private School' (in *The Oxford Book of Caribbean Short Stories*, 1999) revolves around the central event of Denise's humiliation in front of her classmates. If you find a central idea, does this in any way affect one of the characters or does it have the potential to do so? Or, should it have affected a character? Does this central idea have any connection with the end of the story or the title? If the central moment sets up a crisis of some kind, is this resolved for the character? Scrutinise the meanings of this central moment in detail, as in the analysis of 'I Spy' on page 104. Expect ambiguity.

- Look for ideas or images that contrast with this central idea. How does the writer present this contrast? For example, does it have particular consequences for one of the characters? Are there repeated images that reinforce the idea? For example, in 'Miss Brill' (see pages 83–87) what images of the other characters are presented and how do these contrast with a reader's view of Miss Brill?

- How is the narrative constructed around the central idea? In particular, how does the writer control time in the story? Is there, for example, a narrator through whom the events are reported and who cuts across time? Does the story present one continuous scene or does it range across several connected events, as for example, in Joyce's 'The Sisters' or several of Munro's stories. What is it that holds the events together?

- Does the story borrow from any other genre of story or writing? For example, Janet Frame's 'The Terrible Screaming' (in *You Are Now Entering the Human Heart*, 1983) signals that it is an **allegory** in the sentence, '… one day a stranger arrived from a foreign shore', and by identifying the characters by roles such as 'The Distinguished Stranger'. Look out for the use of letters, newspaper articles, diaries and the effects these might have on themes in the story. It is particularly common for short stories to borrow from oral stories.

- What does the story not have? Throughout this book the idea of omission has featured repeatedly. As the genre has developed and readers of short stories have become more and more sophisticated, writers have been able to play on their expectations by leaving out conventional elements of story. For example, Katherine Anne Porter's story 'He' (1930) does not have a central moment at which a character gains some important insight. There is no one moment that has significance for the rest of the story. In this case you must look for something else. The next question to ask is: what state of affairs does the story reveal? This often revolves around tension or conflict between characters over a third idea.

Making comparisons, finding contexts

Since it is unlikely that you will study only one short story, making comparisons between stories is likely to be an important part of your study. Making comparisons essentially involves contextualising the stories in some way. Contexts have the reputation of limiting the ways in which a text can be read, but they can also liberate the reader. You can discover a context for most writing after initial study: for example, Henry James often wrote about the interaction between British and

Americans – 'the international theme' – a theme that was obviously influenced by James' personal circumstances and by the time and place in which he was born. But when a writer is juxtaposed with another, it can have the effect of revealing a different context in which to read them both. Alongside Joyce, Carver's work suggests the contexts of portrayal of the working class and alienation. Alongside Munro, a less obvious pairing, the context of marital relationships in the late 20th century suggests itself, and both Munro and Carver would need to be seen in the context of attitudes to marriage at that time.

Contextualising means introducing a third element that can be used to compare the stories or the writers. Here are some examples from writers mentioned in this book:

- the position of women in late 19th-century America (Chopin, Gilman)
- censorship at the turn of the 19th/20th centuries (Chopin, Joyce)
- gender in early 20th-century stories (Hemingway, Lawrence, Mansfield)
- versions of modernism in short stories (Hemingway, Woolf, Mansfield, Faulkner)
- race and alienation (Gordimer, Naipaul)
- the psychological perspective (James 'The Jolly Corner', Stevenson 'Dr Jekyll and Mr Hyde', Conrad 'The Secret Sharer')
- cutting down to the marrow (the styles of Hemingway and Carver)
- alienation in urban landscapes (Joyce and Carver)
- love stories (Hardy, Munro)
- experiments in capturing consciousness (Woolf, Faulkner)
- making the most out of the ordinary (Woolf, Mansfield, Hemingway, Carver)
- race relations (Gordimer, Kipling)
- middle-age crisis (Munro, Mansfield)

▶ By rereading sections of Part 1 about specific authors, suggest ways in which these authors could be paired, using the above list as a model.

Using the critics

The views of critics of modern short stories come in two forms: (a) the critical approaches to short stories as discussed in Part 4; and (b) the critical readings of individual stories and authors.

(a) These approaches can be used as a guideline and help to give your study of the short story distinctiveness to the genre. It is best to apply these approaches critically, using your own reading of the stories to assess the usefulness of the theories.

If you find that a story cannot easily be categorised or seems to reinvent some of the rules, don't struggle to make it fit a particular theory. You will find, for example, that some stories have no epiphany, no frontier experience, no twist, no plot. This very lack may be your starting point in looking for something else, usually patterns of ideas. It is always useful to consider, for example, especially when reading post-modern stories, that the writer is playing with what the reader might expect from a conventional story. See, for example, the story 'Snow' on pages 92–93. In these cases, it is a good idea to allow some free rein to your personal expectations if these can then be informed by the ideas in this book. Ultimately, remember that the critical approaches are tools rather than ends in themselves.

(b) Critical readings can be used in two connected ways. Use the critics' views to help you read the short story by finding evidence to support what the critic has said. But also use the text of the story to read what the critic has said. In such cases, reading works as a two-way process. You can also use different critics' views against each other in the same way.

▶ To illustrate this two-way process, read the extract from Kipling's 'Lispeth' on pages 80–81, paying attention to:

- the way that Lispeth speaks and acts
- the author's attitude towards the Chaplain's wife
- the way that religion is presented
- the possible meanings of the last two paragraphs.

Now use your reading of 'Lispeth' to read Walter Allen's remarks from *The Short Story in English* (1963):

> 'Lispeth' is at once objective and compassionate, a study of mutually uncomprehending racial codes and of Anglo-Saxon hypocrisy. Here it is worth while pointing out that Kipling's attitude towards misalliance between the races, in which his sympathy goes out especially towards the coloured partner, the woman, is markedly compassionate.

Thus, critical reading should take you repeatedly from the text you are studying to the critic, and then back to the text – until you have worked out your own independent position. But you can also attempt to read the critics using the context in which they were writing to challenge their arguments. Thus, Allen's remarks are betrayed by the word 'coloured' (implying that white is the norm), and by the unusually sympathetic view of Kipling's politics which may have been influenced by the liberalism of the 1960s. A brief look at secondary sources will show that throughout much of the 20th century Kipling's unpopularity was partly due to his association with right wing politics. Clearly, some of the descriptions in 'Lispeth' appear racist today, and it is hard for a present-day reader to reconcile this with the compassion that Allen describes.

Assignments

1   Frank O'Connor believes that short stories are about isolated individuals who undergo a 'frontier experience' (see page 106). With reference to about six short stories you have read, how useful do you find O'Connor's theory?

2   Some critics feel that the idea of epiphany as a moment of insight is a gross oversimplification and that most modern short stories are about lack of insight. With reference to a range of stories that you are studying, write a response to the above opinion.

3   Do you agree that both the frontier theory and epiphany theory are reductionist and therefore cannot do justice to the individual power of stories? Explore this question with reference to several stories.

4   Read some of the stories by the pairs of authors in the list on page 114, or by authors you paired in the task which followed. Test out your ideas and develop them into an extended essay.

6 | Resources

Further reading

Anthologies

Bleiman, Barbara, and Broadbent, Sabrina (eds.) *Headless and Other Stories* (The English and Media Centre, 1996)

Bradbury, Malcolm (ed.) *The Penguin Book of British Short Stories* (Penguin Books, 1988)

Brown, Stewart and Wickham, John (eds.) *The Oxford Book of Caribbean Short Stories* (Oxford University Press, 1999)

Dolley, Christopher (ed.) *The Penguin Book of English Short Stories* (Penguin Books, 1967)

Fadiman, Clifton (ed.) *The World of the Short Story: A 20th Century Collection* (Pan Books, 1986)

Ford, Richard (ed.) *The Granta Book of the American Short Story* (Granta Books, 1992)

Hill, Susan (ed.) *The Penguin Book of Modern Women's Short Stories* (Penguin Books, 1991)

Hunter, Jim (ed.) *Modern Short Stories Two* (Faber and Faber, 1994)

Myszor, Frank (ed.) *Moments of Madness: One Hundred and Fifty Years of Short Stories* (Cambridge University Press, 1997)

Shapard, Robert and Thomas, James (eds.) *Sudden Fiction: American Short Short Stories (*Penguin Books, 1988)

Shapard, Robert and Thomas, James (eds.) *Sudden Fiction International (*Penguin Books, 1991)

Wevers, Lydia (ed.) *New Zealand Short Stories* (Oxford University Press, 1984)

On individual writers of the short story

Blodgett, E.D. *Alice Munro* (Twayne Publishers, Boston, 1988)

Boddy, Gillian *Katherine Mansfield: The Woman and the Writer* (Penguin Books, 1988)

Brady, Kristin *The Short Stories of Thomas Hardy* (Macmillan, London, 1982)

Campbell, Ewing *Raymond Carver: A Study of the Short Fiction* (Twayne Publishers, New York, 1995)

Dick, Susan *Virginia Woolf* in *Modern Fiction Series* (Hodder and Stoughton, 1989)

Head, Dominic *Nadine Gordimer* (Cambridge University Press, 1994)

Karl, Frederick R. *William Faulkner: American Writer* (Faber, 1989)

Sage, Lorna (ed.) *Flesh and the Mirror: Essays on the Art of Angela Carter* (Virago, 1994)

Showalter, Elaine *The Female Malady: Women, Madness and English Culture, 1830–1980* (Virago, 1987)

Steinman, Michael *Frank O'Connor at Work* (Syracuse University Press, 1990)

Thomas, Deborah *Dickens and the Short Story* (Pennsylvania University Press, 1982)

Widdowson, Peter (ed.) *D.H. Lawrence* in *Longman Critical Readers* (Longman, 1992)

Critical studies of the short story

Allen, Walter *The Short Story in English* (Clarendon Press, Oxford, 1981)
Comprehensive coverage of the 20th century, but no theoretical underpinning.

Bates, H.E. *The Modern Short Story from 1809 to 1953* (Evensford Publications, 1941)
A readable introduction the 19th century and modernist eras.

Bloom, Harold *How to Read and Why* (Fourth Estate, 2000)
A 'history' of literature with a substantial section on short stories.

Bonheim, Helmut *The Narrative Modes: Techniques of the Short Story*
(D.S. Brewer, Cambridge, 1982)
A useful technical reference book; thorough but mechanical.

Fowler, Alastair *A History of English Literature* (Blackwell, 1987)
An excellent contextualisation of the modern short story within literary history.

Head, Dominic *The Modernist Short Story* (Cambridge University Press, 1992)
Challenging chapters on major modernists; a useful critique of epiphany.

Levi, Andrew *The Culture and Commerce of the American Short Story* (Cambridge
University Press, 1993)
A useful authoritative guide to a neglected angle, particularly strong on Poe and
magazines.

May, Charles (ed.) *The New Short Story Theories* (Ohio University Press, 1994)
A wide range of invaluable papers on the short story.

O'Connor, Frank *The Lonely Voice: A Study of the Short Story* (The World
Publishing Company, Cleveland, 1963)
A classic study covering the masters and the theory.

O'Donoghue, Bernard 'Getting Started: The Short Story' in *The English Review,*
Vol. 3, Issue 1 (September 1992)
A basic introduction.

O'Faolain, Sean *The Short Story* (The Devin-Adair Co., New York, 1951)
A writer's view, not based on critical theory.

Reid, Ian *The Short Story* in *The Critical Idiom Series* (Methuen, 1977)
A compact introduction to the roots of the short story and major issues.

Shaw, Valerie *The Short Story: A Critical Introduction* (Longman, 1983)
Probably the best available in its coverage and perceptiveness.

Sims, R.J. *The Short Story* in *Brodie's Notes* (Pan Books, 1991)
Very useful at an introductory level.

Websites

Bibliomania: texts of 700 complete short stories
http://www.bibliomania.com/ShortStories/

Classic Short Stories – complete texts
http://www.short-stories.co.uk

The Victorian Web
http://landow.stg.brown.edu/victorian/

Caribbean Literature
http://www.hwcn.org/~aa462/cariblit.html

Raymond Carver
http://www.geocities.com/Athens/Delphi/9020/carver.html

William Faulkner on the Web
http://www.mcsr.olemiss.edu/~egjbp/faulkner/faulkner.html

Thomas Hardy
http://www.geocities.com/hardyshortstories/

Hemingway – The Hemingway Resource Centre
http://www.lostgeneration.com/hrc.htm

Alice Munro
http://members.aol.com/MunroAlice/

Edgar Allan Poe
http://www.poedecoder.com/Qrisse/

Glossary

Allegory   a story that conceals an underlying story with a moral attached. It is usually contrasted with realism.

Art story   a story written as an artistic work rather than purely as a piece of entertainment; not popular or pulp fiction.

Cataphoric reference   the use of a pronoun before its referent rather than the reverse, which is the usual order in English. For a survey of its use in short story openings see 'He Came into her Line of Vision Walking Backwards: Nonsequential Sequence-signals in Short Story Openings' (*Language Learning*, Vol XV, 1965)

Compression   a style of short story writing that emphasises brevity whilst implying a lot more; the opposite of expansion.

Ellipsis   originally a grammatical term, ellipsis refers in this context to the omission of information or of a conventional part of a story.

Epiphany   a term introduced by James Joyce and referring to a moment of insight around which many short stories hinge. The concept has recently been questioned by critics such as Dominic Head.

Exposition   traditionally the opening section of a story in which a situation is laid out. It is usually descriptive and the time span is often broader than in the rest of the story. The end of the exposition might be signalled with words such as 'One day …'.

Framing device   the means by which a short story writer links the beginning and end of a story, thus seeming to frame it. The most common device is to introduce a story teller at the beginning, allow him to tell his story, and return to him at the end.

Frontier   in short story theory this refers to the border between two states. The states can be physical, mental, maturational, emotional and so forth. According to Frank O'Connor, short stories are often about this transition between the two states.

Intertextuality   a philosophical concept that says that all texts are interconnected. Stories build on texts that have gone before, sometimes by means of a specific reference (for example, biblical) or by consciously rewriting an earlier work (for example, Joyce Carol Oates' reworking of James' *The Turn of the Screw*.

Irony   this occurs when the opposite happens to what is expected. In short stories there is often an ironic twist at the end in which there is a dramatic reversal, the outcome of which contrasts with characters' or readers' expectations.

Local colourist   a writer who writes about a local region, helping to create a character for that region.

Magic realism   a form of writing in which fantastic or absurd things happen, but which are treated as if real. In Britain the chief exponent was Angela Carter.

Metafiction   a story that is about some aspect of stories. Such stories are said to be self-conscious because they draw attention to their own status as fictional constructs.

Omniscient narrator   a storyteller who can enter the consciousness of any of the characters and appears as a controlling force behind the action of the story. The omniscient narrator may appear in the story as 'I'. Gradually replaced during the 20th century by multiple voices.

Plot   a term that many have sought to define, but used in this context to mean a series of linked events building sequentially to form a coherent story. It contrasts with stories in which events happen without appearing to lead anywhere.

Realism   a style of writing focusing on everyday life rather than extraordinary events, it purports to show the truth directly. It became popular during the 19th century

Reductionism   the tendency for explanations or theories to reduce processes to their most basic elements. In psychology it refers to the tendency to reduce experiences to mathematical formulae. Literary theories that break fiction down into fixed categories could be said to be reductionist.

Short story cycle   a sequence of connected stories published in book form. Famous examples include *Dubliners* (Joyce), *Winesburg, Ohio* (Anderson) and *The Beggar Maid* (Munro). It is sometimes referred to as whole book fiction.

Sketch   this is a form of writing that pre-dates the modern short story. It may comprise some narrative, but may also be primarily descriptive and contain some reflection on an idea or issue.

Slice of life   a term used to describe stories without a conventionally structured plot, realistically written and often without a conclusive ending. The earliest exponent of this kind of story was Chekhov.

Stream of consciousness   an experimental form of writing begun in the early decades of the 20th century. It aims to capture a person's inner life, especially as it is lived from day to day. It frequently broke the rules by, for example, disregarding conventional punctuation.

Structuralist critics   critics who emphasise the text as a self-contained system of inter-related units. They tend to break the text down into pre-existing categories using an almost mathematical approach to the study of literature.

Tale   this short form emphasises plot and frequently contains conventional elements such as stock characters at the expense of realism.

Unity of impression   a term coined by Poe in the 1840s and suggesting the tightness with which short stories should weave together every word to create a single effect, as preconceived by the writer.

Unreliable narrator   a narrator whose version of the events of the story cannot be trusted. A famous example is the narrator of Henry James' *The Turn of the Screw*.

Chronology

Date	Historical/cultural events	Literary events relevant to short stories
1600		Joseph Addison (1672–1719); Richard Steele (1672–1729)
1750–64	Industrial Revolution in Britain	Walpole *The Castle of Otranto* – first gothic novel
1798		Wordsworth and Coleridge *Lyrical Ballads* – first Romantic poetry
1820		Irving *Sketch Book*
1826	Photography invented	
1835–36		Dickens *Sketches by Boz*
1837	Beginning of Victorian era	
1842		Poe's review of Hawthorne's *Twice-Told Tales*; Gogol 'The Overcoat'
1846		Turgenev *The Sportsman's Sketches*; Thackeray *The Book of Snobs*; Poe 'The Cask of Amontillado'
1860	Start of Impressionism in fine art	
1861–65	American Civil War	
1870	Abolition of slavery in U.S.	
1871	Darwin's theory of evolution	Maupassant 'The Necklace'
1885		Stevenson 'Markheim'
1888		Hardy *Wessex Tales*; Kipling *Plain Tales from the Hills*
1891	Change in U.S. copyright laws	
1892		Perkins Gilman 'The Yellow Wallpaper'
1894–97		*The Yellow Book*
1895	First silent films; Marx's Communist manifesto	
1897		Chopin *A Night in Acadie*; Crane 'The Open Boat'
1899		Chekhov 'Lady with Lapdog'
1900	Freud's theory of the unconscious	
1901	Death of Queen Victoria	
1904		Kipling 'Mrs Bathurst'; first stories from *Dubliners* written

Date	Historical/cultural events	Literary events relevant to short stories
1905		James 'The Jolly Corner'
1912		Conrad 'The Secret Sharer'
1914		Joyce *Dubliners*; Lawrence 'The Prussian Officer'
1914–18	First World War	
1918		Mansfield 'Prelude'
1919		Anderson *Winesburg Ohio*; Woolf 'Kew Gardens'
1920s	Many American writers live in Paris: 'The Lost Generation'	
1925		Hemingway *In Our Time*
1928	Women gain the vote in Britain	
1930s	The Depression	
1939–45	Second World War	
1941		Welty 'Clytie'
1942		Faulkner *Go Down Moses*
1944		Bowen 'The Mysterious Kor'
1948	Apartheid era in South Africa begins	
1949		Gordimer *Face to Face*
1950s	Beginning of migration from Caribbean colonies to Britain	
1959		Naipaul *Miguel Street*
1960s	Revival of women's movement	
1969		Coover 'The Babysitter'
1974		Pritchett 'The Camberwell Beauty'
1979		Carter *The Bloody Chamber*
1982		Narayan *Malgudi Days*
1983		Carver *Cathedral*
1988		Death of Carver; Shappard and Thomas (eds.) *Sudden Fiction*
1991	End of apartheid regime in South Africa	Gordimer *Jump*
1993		Atwood *Good Bones*
1998		Munro *The Love of a Good Woman*
2000		Trevor *The Hill Bachelors*

Index

Irving, Washington 11, 12
Jacobs, W.W. 29
James, Henry 8, 23, 25, 28–29, 35, 113–114; *The Turn of the Screw* 8, 27; 'The Jolly Corner' 27, 29; 'The Real Thing' 29
Joyce, James 28, 30–32, 103, 114; *Dubliners* 30–32; paralysis 31; 'Clay' 32; 'An Encounter' 32; 'Eveline' 102
Kincaid, Jamaica 'My Mother' 48, 72–73 (Extract 6)
Kipling, Rudyard 19, 20–22, 115–116; 'Lispeth' 80–81, 115; 'Mrs Bathurst' 21, 24
Lawrence, D.H. 36–37, 'Tickets Please!' 36, 37, 81–83
local colourists 24, 122
magazines 13, 14, 17, 18, 22, 23, 27
magic realism 42, 48, 51–52, 122
Mais, Roger 'Red Dirt Don't Wash' 72 (Extract 4)
Mansfield, Katherine 30, 37–39, 56, 109, 111; 'The Life of Ma Parker' 38; 'The Daughters of the Late Colonel' 38; 'Prelude' 38; 'At the Bay' 38; 'Bliss' 39; 'Miss Brill' 83–87, 105–106, 113; 'The Fly' 112
Mathews, Brander 103, 110
Maugham, Somerset 41
Maupassant, Guy de 7, 15–16, 21–22; 'The Necklace' 15, 16, 101
May, Charles 47, 105
McKenzie, Aliecia 112
metafiction 42, 122
modernism 18, 20, 27, 29, 30–40, 58
Munro, Alice 8, 49–51, 114; 'Red Dress – 1946' 49; 'Day of the Butterfly' 49; 'Cortes Island' 50; 'The Love of a Good Woman' 50; 'A Wilderness Station' 50
Naipaul, V.S. 48, 63, 68; 'The Nightwatchman's Occurrence Book' 48, 63, 68
Narayan, R.K. 48, 58
Oates, Joyce Carol 10
O'Connor, Flannery 41
O'Connor, Frank 35, 41, 54, 106–108; *The Lonely Voice* 106
omniscient narrator 27, 122

photography 24
plot 11, 59–60, 122
Poe, Edgar Allan 7, 8, 10, 11, 12, 13–15, 16, 21–22, 56–57, 67, 101, 102, 103; The Pit and the Pendulum' 15; 'The Tell–Tale Heart' 15, 76–80; 'The Cask of Amontillado' 15, 71–72 (Extract 3)
Porter, Katherine Anne 41, 113
post-colonialism 47–49
post-modernism 42–43, 59
Pritchett, V.S. 41, 68
reader-oriented criticism 108
realism 10, 23–24, 122
reductionist 108, 122
repetition 68
Romanticism 10
'Saki' (H.H. Munro) 29, 67
serialisation 22–23
short story: beginnings 60–61; Caribbean 47–48; cataphoric reference 61, 121; and the commercial world 22–23, 39; definition of 7–9; and novels 63–64; point of view in 56–57, 67; short short stories 52–53, 55; short story cycles 18, 122; showing and telling 57–58; summary of events 66–67; symbolic endings 65; metaphors for 100–101
Simpson, Hilary 37
sketch 11, 123
slice of life 17, 26, 123
Steele, Richard 11
Stevenson, Robert Louis 19–20; *Dr Jekyll and Mr Hyde* 19, 27; 'Markheim' 72 (Extract 5)
stream of consciousness 29, 123
structuralism 101–102, 123
tales 11, 18, 123
Turgenev, Ivan 12, 16
twist 15, 17, 18, 67
unity of impression 15, 101, 123
unreliable narrator 27, 58, 123
Welty, Eudora 41
Wharton, Edith 24–25
Wollstonecraft, Mary 'Crazy Robin' 12, 73–76
Woolf, Virginia 30, 32–33, 58; 'Kew Gardens' 33; 'The Haunted House' 33

Acknowledgements

The author and publishers wish to thank the following for permission to use copyright material:

Curtis Brown Ltd, London, on behalf of the Estate of the author and Alfred A. Knopf, a division of Random House, Inc for an extract from Elizabeth Bowen 'Maria' from *The Cat Jumps* by Elizabeth Bowen and *The Collected Stories of Elizabeth Bowen*. Copyright © Elizabeth Bowen 1934, copyright © 1981 by Curtis Brown Ltd, Literary Executors of the Estate of Elizabeth Bowen; HarperCollins Publishers and Alfred A Knopf, a division of Random House, Inc for extracts from Raymond Carver 'Cathedral' [also entitled 'Preservation']. Copyright © 1983 by Raymond Carver; International Creative Management, Inc on behalf of the author for Ann Beattie 'Snow' from *Where You'll Find Me* by Ann Beattie, Simon & Schuster (1986). Copyright © 1983 by Ann Beattie; Rogers, Coleridge & White Ltd on behalf of the Estate of the author for an extract from Angela Carter 'The Snow Child' from *The Bloody Chamber* by Angela Carter, Victor Gollancz (1979). Copyright © Angela Carter 1979; A.P. Watt Ltd on behalf of The National Trust for Places of Historical Interest or Natural Beauty for an extract from Rudyard Kipling 'Lispeth' from *Plain Tales from the Hills* by Rudyard Kipling; and on behalf of Felix Licensing, BV with Farrar Straus and Giroux LLC for Nadine Gordimer 'Once Upon a Time' from *Jump and Other Stories* by Nadine Gordimer. Copyright © 1991 by Felix Licensing, BV.

Every effort has been made to reach copyright holders; the publishers would like to hear from anyone whose rights they have unknowingly infringed.